D0114576

THE DISTAFF MUSE

Uniform with this volume

VINTAGE VERSE

THE PLEASURES OF POVERTY

THE DISTAFF MUSE

An Anthology of Poetry written by Women

COMPILED BY

CLIFFORD BAX

AND

MEUM STEWART

LONDON

HOLLIS & CARTER

1949

PRINTED IN GREAT BRITAIN BY THE BOWERING PRESS, PLYMOUTH
FOR HOLLIS & CARTER, LTD.,
25 ASHLEY PLACE,
LONDON, S.W.1

First published 1949

WE DEDICATE OUR SHARE OF THIS BOOK
TO THE MINIATURIST
LISA DE MONTFORT
C.B.
M.S.

PREFATORY NOTE

by Meum Stewart

IN MY HAMPSTEAD garden on a gentle summer evening Clifford Bax and I discussed a paper which he had been invited to read 'over the air'. It was to be called *Feminine Poetry*: a difficult theme to compress into twenty minutes. In the end there was what I can only call 'an emotional hitch' in the Poetry Department at Broadcasting House. Nevertheless, that unread paper was the origin of this book. We decided to make a book of the poetry written by women and, in order that it might figure as a Companion-of-Honour to *Vintage Verse*, Messrs. Hollis & Carter were asked to sponsor it. They agreed, and while my collaborator was to supply the running commentary, I was to share the adventure by searching for the best feminine poems available.

As a result I spent many happy hours in the London Library and the British Museum, and it was with pride in the work of my sex that, when the collection was completed, I realised what an impressive number of poets of quality we had brought together, especially in the large modern section.

Various contributors rebelled against the proposed title, *Feminine Poetry*, and when our Publishers upheld this objection, we consented to change the title, although we could not withdraw our contention that the poetry of women ought to be distinguishable from the poetry of men. No woman objects to being told that she has 'feminine hands'. Indeed, if there were no difference between the poetry written by the two sexes, there could be no purpose in segregating the poetry written by women. I puzzled for a long time over so marked a revulsion from the words 'Feminine Poetry', and then, suddenly, I perceived that the objections of our contributors came from writers of a certain age-group. Perhaps I should say that I belong to that age-group myself, and I well remember how in the Nineteen-Twenties, when talk over studio fires was concerned with literature, praise was never given to a woman unless it could be said 'She writes like a man'. These women had all grown up in the patronising aura of the male, and now, when the young were unconscious of and unaffected by their long struggle for equality, Clifford Bax and I were about to topple over the carefully-built edifice and show that women not only write like women, but had that to say in their poetry which no man could or would try to express. They were convinced we were out to prove them inferior. How very different our intention was, we hope the reader will realise.

I have found my own sex courageous and stoical; idealistic yet realistic; pitifully quick to feel change in love's colour, and quicker still to forgive; always sensitive to beauty and perceptive of the life around them; and almost without exception mystically conscious of 'another world than this'. You who read will, I think, find all these qualities expressed somewhere or other in the pages of this book.

March, 1948. M. S.

CONTENTS

ACKNOWLEDGMENTS

THE LIST OF acknowledgments is a long one. We have to thank the following:

Mr. Seumas MacManus for the late Ethna Carbery; The Executors of Mary Coleridge; Messrs. Ernest Benn Ltd. for Michael Field (*Wild Honey*); Messrs. Longmans Green & Co. Ltd. and The Executors of Eva Selina Gore-Booth (*Selected Poems*); Virginia Graham and Messrs. Jonathan Cape Ltd. (*Consider the Years*); The Executors of Lady Gregory; Nora Hopper and Messrs. John Lane, The Bodley Head (*Ballads in Prose*); Laurence Hope and Messrs. William Heinemann Ltd. (*The Garden of Kama*); Wrenne Jarman and *John o'London's*, also *The R.A.F. Quarterly*; The Hon. Kathleen Lawless for the late Hon. Emily Lawless; Eiluned Lewis and The Society of Authors (*Morning Song and Other Poems*); Lilian Bowes-Lyon and Messrs. Jonathan Cape Ltd. (*A Rough Walk Home*); J. Middleton Murry and The Society of Authors for the late Katherine Mansfield; R. A. French for the late Susan Mitchell; Ruth Pitter and The Cresset Press (*The Spirit Watches*); Messrs. Elkin Matthews & Marrot for Dollie Radford; Kathleen Raine and Messrs. Nicholson & Watson (*Stone and Flower* and *Living in Time*); Anne Ridler and Messrs. Faber & Faber (*The Nine Bright Shiners*), also the Oxford University Press (*Poems*); Joyce Rowe and The Favil Press (*She Died Alive*); Margot Ruddock and Messrs. J. M. Dent & Sons Ltd. (*The Lemon Tree*); The Hon. Victoria Sackville-West and Leonard and Virginia Woolf of the Hogarth Press (*Collected Poems*); E. J. Scovell and Messrs. George Routledge & Sons (*A Midsummer Meadow*); Dora Sigerson Shorter and Messrs. Constable & Co. Ltd. (*The Sad Years*); Helen Spalding and Messrs. Methuen (*What Images Return*); Stevie Smith and Messrs. Jonathan Cape Ltd. (*Tender Only to One*); Muriel Stuart and Messrs. Heinemann Ltd. (*Poems*); Miss Pamela Hinkson for the late Katharine Tynan; Helen Waddell and Messrs. Constable & Co. Ltd. (*Medieval Latin Lyrics*); The Trustees of the Mary Webb Estate and Messrs. Jonathan Cape Ltd. (*Poems* and *The Spring of Joy*); Anna Wickham and The Richards Press (*The Man with a Hammer*); Margaret Willy and Messrs. Chatersons Ltd. (*The Invisible Sun*); also the *Observer* and *Country Life*; Ursula Wood and Messrs. Basil Blackwell (*No Other Choice*); Margaret L. Woods and Messrs. John Lane, The Bodley Head, (*Collected Poems*).

Also to Jane Barton, Vera Bax, Horatia Calverley, Frances Cornford, Mary W. Findlater, Eleanor Farjeon, Kathleen Hewitt, F. Tennyson Jesse, Olga Katzin, Joan Lamburn, Alice Milligan, Moira O'Neill, Irene Rathbone (*Was there a Summer?*, published Constable & Co. Ltd.), Phyllis Reid, The Hon. Victoria Sackville-West, Fiona Stewart, Sylvia Townsend Warner, Dorothy Wellesley (the Duchess of Wellington) and Antonia White.

We tender our apologies to Winifred Welles and The Executors of Violet Fane, with whom we have not been able to get into touch.

C. B. and M. S.

PART ONE

Part One

SINCE THE TASTE of experience from the beginning to the end of life is conditioned by the sex with which we are born, I believe that a woman's verse or prose ought to be as recognisably feminine as her handwriting is and that, if it is not, then something has gone awry.

Have women nothing distinctly their own which they can add to our literature? Ought both men and women to express themselves as though they were neuters? That, apparently, is the ideal of certain persons, but if there were no sex distinction in literature we should be, as in life itself, immeasurably the poorer. Fortunately it is only mediocre writers who can write as if they were neuters.

It may have been possible to suppose that the novels of 'George Eliot' were written by a man, but it would have been useless for Jane Austen to seek cover under the pseudonym of 'Napoleon Power'. Happily for the world she made full use of her feminine assets.

This having been firmly stated, because I firmly believe it, let us begin the book with an extract from a poem which, according to Professor Skeat, 'could not have been written earlier than 1450'. For this reason he removed it from the canon of Chaucer's Works, Chaucer having died in 1400. He goes on to say that 'it was probably written, as it purports to be, by a lady. . . . Nothing but a complete ignorance of the history of the English language could attribute the poem to the fourteenth century.'

The subject of this delightful narrative is a tourney between the Knights of the Flower and the Knights of the Leaf, watched by their respective ladies. A storm breaks, and the ladies of the one party not only find shelter for the other ladies but also see to the drying of their clothes. As the Professor has indicated, one of these ladies—toward the end of the poem—addresses the author as one woman to another. This, of course, might well be contrived by a man's imagination, but Skeat supports his divination with the following passage:

> 'The most characteristic thing is the continual reference to colours, dresses, ornaments, and decorations. In (the Flower) we have de-

scriptions of, or reference to, white surcoats, velvet, seams, emeralds, purfils, colours, sleeves, trains, pearls, diamonds, a fret of gold, chaplets of leaves, chaplets of woodbine, chaplets of *agnus-castus*, a crown of gold, thundering trumpets, the treasury of Prester John, white cloaks, chaplets of oak, banners of Tartary silk, more pearls, collars, escutcheons, kings-of-arms, cloaks of white cloth, crowns set with pearls, rubies, sapphires, and diamonds. Then there is a company all clad in one suit (or livery); heralds and pursuivants, more chaplets and escutcheons, men in armour with cloth of gold and horse-trappings, with bosses on their bridles and peitrels—it is surely needless to go on, though we have only arrived at line 246.'

1 The Flower and the Leaf.[1] *(Anonymous) c.* 1450

(lines 127 to 189)

And as I sat, the briddes[2] herkning thus,
Me thought that I herd voices sodainly,
The most sweetest and most delicious
That ever any wight, I trow trewly,
Herde in his lyf, for (that) the armony
And sweet accord was in so good musyk,
That the voice to angels most was lyk.

At the last, out of a grove even by,
That was right goodly and plesaunt to sight,
I sy[3] where there cam singing lustily
A world of ladies; but to tell aright
Their greet beautè, it lyth not in my might,
Ne their array; nevertheless, I shal
Tell you a part, though I speke not of al.

In surcotes whyte, of veluet wel sitting,
They were (y)clad; and the semes echoon[4],
As it were a maner garnishing,
Was set with emeraudes, oon and oon,

[1] The words or part-words in brackets were added by Skeat.
[2] birds [3] sy = saw. [4] each one.

By and by; but many a riche stoon
Was set (up-)on the purfils, out of dout,
Of colours, sleves, and traines round about;

As gret(e) perles, round and orient,
Diamondes fyne and rubies rede,
And many another stoon, of which I want
The names now; and everich[1] on her hede,
A riche fret of gold, which, without drede,
Was ful of statly riche stones set;
And every lady had a chapelet

On her hede, of (leves) fresh and grene,
So wel (y-)wrought, and so mérveilously,
That it was a noble sight to sene;
Some of laurer, and some ful plesauntly
Had chapelets of woodbine, and sadly
Some of *agnus-castus*[2] ware also
Chapelets fresh; but there were many tho

That daunced and eek song ful soberly;
But all they yede[3] in maner of compas.
But oon ther yede in-mid the company
Sole by her-self; but al folowed the pace
(Which) that she kept, whos hevenly-figured face
So plesaunt was, and her wel-shape persòn,
That of beautè she past hem everichon.

And more richly beseen, by manifold,
She was also, in every maner thing;
On her hede, ful plesaunt to behold,
A crowne of gold, rich for any king;
A braunch of *agnus-castus* eek bering
In her hand; and, to my sight, trewly,
She lady was of (al) the company.

[1] everyone.
[2] *agnus-castus*: 'a verbinaceous shrub with blue or white flowers.'
[3] yede = went.

And she began a roundel lustily,
That *Sus le foyl de vert moy* men call,
Seen, et mon joly cuer endormi;[1]
And than the company answéred all
With voice(s) swete entuned and so small,
That me thought it the sweetest melody
That ever I herde in my lyf, soothly.

And thus they came(n), dauncing and singing,
Into the middes of the mede echone,
Before the herber, where I was sitting,
And, god wot, me thought I was wel bigon;
For that I might avyse hem, on and on,
Who fairest was, who coud best dance or sing,
Or who most womanly was in al thing.

Elizabeth of York: 1465–1503

This high-born lady was soon the centre of much political disturbance. She was a daughter of Edward the Fourth and Elizabeth Woodville. Richard the Third is said to have wished to marry her, probably for political reasons; but in 1486 she married Henry the Seventh and in 1487 she was crowned Queen of England. She was thought to have died of grief on account of the death of her son, Prince Arthur. Her personality must have been attractive or Sir Thomas More would not have made her death the subject of an elegy.

This poem of happiness is an irregular *sestina*. The *sestina* was an elaborate form invented by the troubadour Arnaut Daniel (twelfth century) who was praised by Dante. The reader will notice that the last six lines of the first stanza in the poem successively form the first lines of the stanzas which follow. 'Twin' means break apart or separate into two. 'A lusty pin' means a strong peg or a stable foundation. Not many poets have declared: 'My joys be double where others' are but thin. . . .'

[1] Skeat says that these two French phrases do not make sense.

2 I Pray to Venus

My heart is set upon a lusty pin;
I pray to Venus of good continuance,
For I rejoice the case that I am in,
Deliver'd from sorrow, annex'd to pleasance,
Of all comfort having abundance;
This joy and I, I trust, shall never twin—
My heart is set upon a lusty pin.

I pray to Venus of good continuance
Since she hath set me in the way of ease;
My hearty service with my attendance
So to continue it ever I may please;
Thus voiding from all pensful disease,
Now stand I whole far from all grievance—
I pray to Venus of good continuance.

For I rejoice the case that I am in,
My gladness is such that giveth me no pain,
And so to sorrow never shall I blynne,
And though I would I may not me refrain;
My heart and I so set 'tis certain
We shall never slake, but ever new begin—
For I rejoice the case that I am in.

Deliver'd from sorrow, annex'd to pleasance,
That all my joy I set as aught of right,
To please as after my simple suffisance
To me the goodliest, most beauteous in sight;
A very lantern to all other light,
Most to my comfort on her remembrance—
Deliver'd from sorrow, annex'd to pleasance.

Of all comfort having abundance,
As when that I think that goodlihead
Of that most feminine and meek countenance
Very mirror and star of womanhead;

Whose right good fame so large abroad doth spread,
Full glad for me to have recognisance—
Of all comfort having abundance.

This joy and I, I trust, shall never twin,
So that I am so far forth in the trace,
My joys be double where others' are but thin,
For I am stably set in such a place,
Where beauty 'creaseth and ever willeth grace,
Which is full famous and born of noble kin—
This joy and I, I trust, shall never twin.

Anne Boleyn: 1507–1536

She, who was 'wild for to hold, though she seem tame', hardly needs a note. If her daughter (Queen Elizabeth) had been a boy, Henry the Eighth might have spared her the executioner's axe. There are several poems, usually laments, attributed to Anne Boleyn (or Bullen) but most of them look like verses written by other persons after her death. Although the following lyric may be of the same kind, it could well have been written by herself because it is simple and it does not over-dramatise her unhappy situation.

3 Cruel Spite

Defilèd is my name full sore,
  Through cruel spite and false report,
That I may say for evermore,
  Farewell, my joy! adieu comfórt!

For wrongfully ye judge of me,—
  Unto my fame a mortal wound.
Say what ye list, it will not be;
  Ye seek for that can not be found.

Queen Elizabeth: 1533–1603

Again, it may be that these verses are an imaginative effort by some other poet, but we know that the great Queen did, like her father, occasionally write verse. The reader will judge whether they seem authentic or not.

4 Self and the Otherself

I grieve; and dare not show my discontent!
I love; and yet am forced to seem to hate!
I do; yet dare not say, I ever meant!
I seem stark mute; but inwardly do prate!
I am, and not; I freeze and yet am burned;
Since from myself, my otherself I turned!

My care is like my shadow in the sun;
Follows me flying! flies, when I pursue it!
Stands and lies by me! doth what I have done!
This too familiar Care doth make me rue it!
Nor means I find, to rid him from my breast,
Till, by the end of things, it be supprest.

Some gentler Passions slide into my mind;
For I am soft, and made of melting snow.
Or be more cruel, Love! and so be kind:
Let me, or float, or sink! be high, or low!
Or let me live with some more sweet content;
Or die! and so forget what Love e'er meant.

Mary Stuart, Queen of Scots: 1542–1587

It was alleged by her Scottish enemies that in a silver-gilt casket which belonged to the Earl of Bothwell, whom Mary had hastily married, they found eleven sonnets, and one that was unfinished, together with eight letters said to have been written by her to Bothwell. The discovery was made, they affirmed, in 1567, and both the letters and the poems were published (by others) during the Queen's lifetime. They have formed matter for controversy ever since. The sonnets are in French, and if they were forged, the fabricator wasted time in laboriously constructing them because they do not incriminate Mary Stuart in the murder of her second husband, Darnley. (At fifteen she had married the French Dauphin who, soon after coming to the Throne, had died.) Those who deny the authenticity of the casket-papers base their defence chiefly on the fact that Mary's enemies never produced the originals, although the Queen challenged them to do so. The casket itself is still in existence—with evidence that the locks were forced. They also quote Brantôme as having reported that the great Ronsard, who had been the Queen's poetry-tutor, considered the sonnets to be unworthy of her skill. Brantôme however is said by some critics not to be an infallible witness.

From internal evidence the poems appear to be obviously genuine. Here indeed are clear examples of a poetry which, I venture to say, no man could have written; nor does the wildness and sincerity of their passion suggest a cool-headed fabricator. Again, the disparaging reference in Sonnet V to Lady Bothwell's poor taste in dress is not at all likely to have emanated from a forger's mind, howsoever ingenious. If the letters and sonnets were fabricated, their inventor would have made them much more incriminating than they are. Even the breaking-off of the unfinished sonnet weighs against the theory or fancy that the poems were not written by the Queen. In the present writer's judgement she did not finish it because Bothwell arrived—to carry her away.

Six Sonnets

I

O you High Gods, have pity, and let me find
  Somehow some incontestable way to prove
  (So that he *must* believe in it) my love
And this unwavering constancy of mind!
Alas, he rules already with no let
  A body and a heart which must endure
  Pain and dishonour in a life unsure,
The obloquy of friends and worse things yet.

  For him I would account as nothing those
  Whom I named friends, and put my faith in foes:
For him I'd let the round world perish, I
  Who have hazarded both conscience and good name,
And, to advance him, happily would die. . . .
  What's left to prove my love always the same?

6

Into his hands, utterly into his power,
I place my son, my life, my honour and all
My Subjects and my country, being in thrall
To him so fast that daily, hour by hour,
My all-surrendered soul hath no intent
But, despite any trouble which may ensue,
To make him see that my great love is true,
And that my constancy is permanent.

Storm or fair weather, let come what come may!
My soul has found its bourne and there shall stay.
Soon will I give him proof beyond all fears
That I am one faithful with no disguise,
And not by feign'd submission or false tears,
As others use, but in quite different wise.

7

(Line 12 probably refers to Bothwell's wedding-day.)

When you so wildly loved her, she was cold;
And when your suffering brought you near to madness,
As comes to all whose love is uncontrolled,
She did but counterfeit a little sadness
That—she could catch no joy from your fierce fire.
Her dresses proved that in her own proud view
No imperfections, howsoever dire,
Could blot her image from a heart so true.
I saw in her no right and proper dread
Lest such a husband, such a man, should die.
You gave her all she is; and she, instead
Of glorying in the hour that sealed your fate,
Has never prized it at its own just rate:
Yet you can say you loved her desperately!

8

That you trust *her*, alas, is plain enough
  And that you doubt *my* truth is all too plain.
O my Sole Wealth and my One Only Love,
  I strive to make you sure of me—in vain:
You think me light, as far too well I see,
  And watch me with suspicion all day long
Though without cause: whereby you do to me,
Dear Heart, a very great and grievous wrong.
You little know what love to you I bear;
  You even fear lest someone else may win me;
You look upon my words as empty air,
  And think my heart is weak as wax within me;
You count me a vain woman without sense:
Yet all you do makes my love more intense.

9

(Lines 4 and 5 refer to an occasion when Mary rode twenty miles in order to visit Bothwell, who had killed an outlaw but had been seriously wounded.)

For him what countless tears I must have shed:
  First, when he made himself my body's lord
  Before he had my heart: and afterward
When I became distraught because he bled
So copiously that almost life went out:
  And at that sight fear seized my heart and head
  Both for the love I bore him and the dread
Of losing my sole rampart and redoubt.
For him I turned my honour to disgrace,
  Though honour is our one sure joy and pride:
For him bade Conscience find a humbler place,
  Chilled my most trusted friends, and set aside
Every consideration! . . . What would I do?
Make a love-compact, Love of my heart, with you!

10

I seek but one thing—to make sure of You
 Who are the sole sustainer of my life;
And if I am presumptuous so to do,
 In spite of all their bitterness and strife,
It is because your gentle Love's one thought
 Is both to love and serve you loyally,
To count the worst that fate can do as naught,
 And to make *my* will with *your* will agree.
Someday you certainly will comprehend
 How steadfast is my purpose and how real,
Which is to do you pleasure until death,
Only to you, being subject: in which faith
I do indeed most fervently intend
To live and die. To this I set my seal.

Margaret Cavendish, Duchess of Newcastle: 1624–1674

At the age of twenty-one, when the Civil War was already dividing the British people, this grave and eccentric lady married the Duke of Newcastle and became a maid-of-honour to the Queen. The Duke wrote various treatises the best known of which is an expert manual of horsemanship. The Duchess and he became patrons of Ben Jonson (in his old age), Shirley, Davenant (reputed to be the son of Shakespeare), Dryden, and the philosopher Thomas Hobbes. They were not passionately political but they sided with the King because, as the Duke said, they hated 'whatsoever was like to disturb the public peace' and because the monarchy was 'the foundation and support of his own greatness'. When the Puritans had achieved victory, the Newcastles forfeited their estates, went into exile and lived in penury at Paris, Rotterdam and Antwerp. Charles the Second restored their estates to them but the Duchess estimated her husband's loss at nearly a million pounds.

At the court of Charles the Second, Margaret Cavendish was disliked and treated as a figure of fun on account of her literary and philosophical pretensions. She is said, for example, to have kept 'a bevy of maids-of-honour obliged to be ready at all hours to "register her Grace's conceptions".' Pepys, who always flowed with the fashion, refers to 'the ridiculous history of my Lord Newcastle writ by his wife, which shows her to be a mad, conceited, ridiculous woman, and he an ass to suffer her to write what she writes *to* him and *of* him'. A better critic—Charles Lamb—said of her work that 'no casket is rich enough, no case sufficiently durable, to honour and keep soft such a jewel'.

11 Mirth and Melancholy

Melancholy

Her voice is low and gives a hollow sound;
She hates the light and is in darkness found
Or sits with blinking lamps, or tapers small,
Which various shadows make against the wall.
She loves nought else but noise which discord makes;
As croaking frogs whose dwelling is in lakes;
The raven's hoarse, the mandrake's hollow groan
And shrieking owls which fly i' the night alone;
The tolling bell, which for the dead rings out;
A mill, where rushing waters run about;
The roaring winds, which shake the cedars tall,
Plough up the seas, and beat the rocks withal.
She loves to walk in the still moonshine night,
And in a thick dark grove she takes delight;
In hollow caves, thatched houses, and low cells
She loves to live, and there alone she dwells.

Mirth

I dwell in groves that gilt are with the sun;
Sit on the banks by which clear waters run;
In summers hot down in a shade I lie,
My music is the buzzing of a fly;
I walk in meadows where grows fresh green grass;
In fields where corn is high I often pass;
Walk up the hills, where round I prospects see,
Some bushy woods, and some all champaigns be;

Returning back, I in fresh pastures go,
To hear how sheep do bleat, and cows do low;
In winter cold, when nipping frosts come on,
Then do I live in a small house alone.

12 Dialogue betwixt Peace and War

PEACE War makes the Vulgar multitude to Drink
In at the Ear, the Foul and muddy sink
Of Factions Tales, by which they Dizzy grow,
That the clear Sight of Truth they do not know,
But Reeling stand, know not what way to take,
And when they chuse, 'tis wrong, for War they make.

WAR Thou Flattering and most Unjust Peace, which draws
The Vulgar by thy Rhet'rick to hard Laws,
Which makes them Silly, and content to be
To take up Voluntary Slavery,
Thou mak'st great Inequalities beside,
Some bear like Asses, some on Horse-back Ride.

PEACE O War, thou Cruel Enemy to Life,
Unquiet Neighbour, breeding always Strife;
Tyrant thou art, to Rest will give no time,
And blessed Peace thou Punish'st as a Crime;
Factions thou mak'st in every Publick weal,
From Bonds of Friendship tak'st off Wax and Seal;
All Natural Affections are by thee
Massacred, none escapes thy Cruelty;
The Root of all Religion thou pull'st up,
Dost every Branch of Ceremony Lop;
Civil Society to Manners base
Thou turn'st, no Laws nor Customs can get place;
Each mind within itself cannot agree,
But all do strive for Superiority:
In the whole world thou dost disturbance make,
To save themselves none knows what ways to take.

WAR O Peace, thou idle Drone, which Lov'st to dwell,
If it but keep them Safe, in a poor Cell;
Thy Life thou Sleep'st away, Thoughts lazy lye:
Sloth buries Fame, makes all great Actions dye.

PEACE I am the Bed of Rest and Couch of Ease,
My conversation doth all Creatures please;
The Parents I'm of Learning and of Arts,
Religion's Nurse and Comfort to all Hearts;
I am the Guardian Virtue safe do keep,
Under my Roof she may securely Sleep;
I am adorn'd with Pastimes and with Sports,
Each several Creature still to me Resorts.

WAR A School am I, where all Men may grow Wise,
For prudent Wisdom in Experience lies;
A Theatre, where Noble Minds do stand,
A Mint of Honour, Coyn'd for Valour's Hand;
I am a Throne, which is for Valour fit,
And a great Court, where Royal Fame may Sit;
A Field in which Ambition much doth run;
Courage still seeks me, Cowards do me shun.

Katherine Philips (Fowler): 1631–1664

Her father was a merchant and presbyterian of London, but his daughter soon transferred her zeal to the cause of King and Church. At sixteen she married a Welshman, and their home in Cardigan became a literary centre. It was here that, in the mode of the period, she was accorded the fancy name of Orinda, soon to be expanded into 'the Matchless Orinda'.

After her husband's death she lived in Dublin, where she translated Corneille's *Pompée*, her version being played with much success at the (Dublin) Smock Alley Theatre. In March 1664 she returned to London and there, in the June of the same year, she died of small-pox.

She was an ardent 'apostle' of friendships between women. Indeed, the 'Lucasia' mentioned so lovingly in *Wiston Vault* was one of her intimates—Anne Owen, afterwards Viscountess Dungannon. The famous Jeremy Taylor dedicated to her a book which has friendship for its theme.

'Wiston' is a sea-coast village in Pembrokeshire. The church, 'restored' in the eighteen-sixties, still exists.

13 Wiston Vault

And why this vault and tomb? Alike we must
Put off distinction, and put on our dust;
Nor can the stateliest fabric help to save
From the corruptions of a common grave,
Nor for the Resurrection more prepare,
Than if the dust were scattered into air.
What then? Th'ambition's just, say some, that we
May thus perpetuate our memory.
Ah, false vain task of art! ah, poor weak man
Whose monument does more than's merit can!
Who by his friends' best care and love's abused,
And in his very epitaph accused;
For did they not suspect his name would fall,
There would not need an epitaph at all.
But after death, too, I would be alive,
And shall, if my Lucasia do survive.
I quit these pomps of death, and am content,
Having her heart to be my monument:
Though ne'er stone to me, 'twill stone for me prove,
By the peculiar miracles of love.
There I'll inscription have which no tomb gives:
Not HERE ORINDA LIES, but, HERE SHE LIVES.

14 Little Hector Philips

(her one (own) little son, born 1655, named after
his Welsh grandfather)

Twice forty months of wedlock I did stay,
Then had my vows crowned with a lovely boy,
And yet in forty days he dropt away:
O swift vicissitude of human joy.

I did but see him and he disappeared,
I did but pluck the rosebud and it fell,
A sorrow unforeseen and scarcely feared:
For ill can mortals their afflictions spell.

And now, sweet babe, what can my trembling heart
Suggest to right my doleful fate or thee?
Tears are my muse, and sorrow all my art,
So piercing groans must be thy elegy.

Thus, whilst no eye is witness of my moan,
I grieve thy loss, ah, boy too dear to live!
And let the unconcernèd world alone,
Who neither will, nor can, refreshment give.

An offering, too, for thy sad tomb I have,
Too just a tribute to thy early hearse:
Receive these gasping numbers to thy grave,
The last of thy unhappy mother's verse.

Aphra Behn (Johnson): 1640–1689

Here is one of the ablest and most enterprising women in the whole of our literary history. Her father was a barber; she was baptized at Wye, in Kent; and was taken in childhood to Surinam (then a British possession) in the West Indies. At the age of eighteen she returned to England and soon afterwards married a London merchant of Dutch extraction. A few years later her husband died, perhaps not having realised that he had married a genius, but during their married life it seems likely that she had mastered the Dutch language. When war with the Dutch broke out, Mrs. Behn was sent as a British spy to Antwerp where, at the end of 1666, she discovered 'the design formed by de Ruyter, in conjunction with the de Witts, of sailing up the Thames and burning the English ships in their harbours' (*Enc. Brit.*). The home authorities pooh-poohed this brilliant example of espionage, and Mrs. Behn, not unnaturally, decided to let them get on by the light of their own intelligence.

Returning to London she had the courage (remarkable indeed in those days) to compete with the playwrights of the time. She and Mrs. Centlivre are the earliest of our women-dramatists, nor does her work suffer by comparison with that of her male contemporaries if we exclude the few that are household-names. She also wrote a still-readable romance about the African Prince Oroonoko and his love Imsinda, based on her memories of Surinam. The following poems show that she had also a lively and graceful gift for lyric-writing.

She was buried 'in the cloisters of Westminster Abbey'. Her dramatic Works were first collected in 1702.

15 A Jolly Swain

From *The City Heiress*; or, *Sir Timothy Treat-All*

Philander was a jolly Swain,
  And lov'd by ev'ry Lass;
Whom when he met along the Plain,
  He laid upon the Grass.

And here he kist, and there he play'd
  With this and then the t'other,
Till every wanton smiling Maid
  At last became a Mother.

And to her Swain, and to her Swain,
  The Nymph begins to yield;
Ruffle, and breathe, then to't again,
  Thou'rt Master of the Field.

16 Amyntas Led Me to a Grove

From *The Dutch Lover*

Amyntas led me to a Grove,
  Where all the trees did shade us;
The Sun itself, tho it had strove,
  Yet could not have betray'd us.
The place secure from human Eyes,
  No other fear allows,
But when the Winds that gently rise
  Do kiss the yielding Boughs.

Down there we sat upon the Moss,
  And did begin to play
A thousand wanton Tricks, to pass
  The Heat of all the Day.
A many Kisses he did give,
  And I return'd the same:
Which made me willing to receive
  That which I dare not name.

His charming Eyes no aid requir'd,
  To tell their amorous Tale;
On her that was already fir'd,
  'Twas easy to prevail.
He did but kiss, and clasp me round,
  Whilst they his thoughts exprest,
And laid me gently on the Ground;
  Oh! who can guess the rest?

17 Love in Fantastick Triumph

From *Abdelazer*; or, *The Moor's Revenge*

LOVE in fantastick Triumph sat,
  Whilst bleeding Hearts around him flow'd,
For whom fresh Pains he did create,
  And strange Tyrannick Pow'r he shew'd;
From thy bright Eyes he took his Fires,
  Which round about in sport he hurl'd;
But 'twas from mine he took Desires,
  Enough t'undo the amorous World.

From me he took his Sighs and Tears,
  From thee his Pride and Cruelty;
From me his Languishments and Fears,
  And ev'ry killing Dart from thee:
Thus thou, and I, the God have arm'd,
  And set him up a Deity;
But my poor Heart alone is harm'd,
  Whilst thine the Victor is, and free.

Anne Finch (Kingsmill), Countess of Winchelsea: 1661–1720

The poetry of Anne Finch may be said to have been disinterred in 1815 by William Wordsworth. He affirmed that no English poetry contained 'a single new image of external nature' between '*Paradise Lost* and Thomson's *Seasons* except Pope's *Windsor Forest* and the Countess's *Nocturnal Reverie*.' Wordsworth, writing to Alexander Dyce in 1830, gives the following criticism:

> 'I observed that Lady Winchelsea was unfortunate in her models PINDARIS and FABLES; nor does it appear from her ARISTOMENES that she would have been more successful than her contemporaries if she had cultivated tragedy. She had sensibility sufficient for the tender parts of dramatic writing, but in the stormy and tumultuous she would probably have failed altogether. She seems to have made it a moral and religious duty to control her feelings lest they should mislead her. I have often applied two lines of her drama to her affections:
>
> Love's soft bands,
> His gentle cords of hyacinths and roses,
> Wove in the dewy Spring when storms are silent.
>
> By the by, in the next page are two impassioned lines spoken to a person fainting:
>
> Then let me hug and press thee into life,
> And lend thee motion from my beating heart.
>
> From the style and versification of this, so much her longest work, I conjecture that Lady Winchelsea had but a slender acquaintance with the drama of the earlier part of the preceding century. Yet her style in rhyme is often *admirable, chaste, tender, and vigorous*, and entirely free from sparkle, antithesis, and that over-culture, which reminds one by its broad glare, its stiffness, and heaviness, of the double daisies of the garden, compared with their modest and sensitive kindred of the fields.'

In 1701 she published a poem called *Spleen*, and twelve years later her *Poems*. Leigh Hunt, seldom if ever at fault, wrote that 'the celebrated *Spleen* still deserves a place on every toilet, male or female'.

18 The Tree

Fair TREE! for thy delightful Shade
'Tis just that some Return be made;
Sure, some Return is due from me
To thy cool Shadows, and to thee.
When thou to BIRDS do'st Shelter give,
Thou Musick do'st from them receive;
If TRAVELLERS beneath thee stay,
Till Storms have worn themselves away,
That Time in praising thee they spend,
And thy protecting Pow'r commend:
The SHEPHERD here, from Scorching freed,
Tunes to thy dancing Leaves his Reed;
Whilst his lov'd Nymph, in Thanks, bestows
Her flow'ry Chaplets on thy Boughs.
Shall I then only Silent be,
And no Return be made by me?
No; let this Wish upon thee wait,
And still to flourish be thy Fate,
To future Ages may'st thou stand
Untouch'd by the rash Workman's hand;
'Till that large Stock of Sap is spent,
Which gives thy Summer's Ornament;
'Till the fierce Winds, that vainly strive
To shock thy Greatness whilst alive,
Shall on thy lifeless Hour attend,
Prevent the Axe, and grace thy End;
Their scatter'd Strength together call,
And to the Clouds proclaim thy Fall;
Who then their Ev'ning-Dews may spare,
When thou no longer art their Care;
But shalt, like ancient Heroes, burn,
And some bright Hearth be made thy Urn.

19 A Letter to Dafnis

April 2nd, 1685

This to the Crown, and blessing of my life,
The much lov'd husband, of a happy wife.
To him, whose constant passion found the art
To win a stubborn, and ungrateful heart;
And to the World, by tend'rest proof discovers
They err, who say that husbands can't be lovers.
With such return of passion, as is due,
Daphnis I love, Daphnis my thoughts pursue,
Daphnis, my hopes, my joys, are bounded all in you:
Ev'n I, for Daphnis, and my promise sake,
What I in women censure, undertake.
But this from love, not vanity, proceeds;
You know who writes; and I who 'tis that reads.
Judge not my passion, by my want of skill,
Many love well, though they express itt ill;
And I your censure cou'd with pleasure bear,
Wou'd you but soon return, and speak itt here.

20 A Song

Love, thou art best of Human Joys,
  Our chiefest Happiness below;
All other Pleasures are but Toys,
Musick without Thee is but Noise,
  And Beauty but an empty Show.

Heav'n, who knew best what Man wou'd move,
  And raise his Thoughts above the Brute;
Said, Let him Be, and Let him Love;
That must alone his Soul improve,
  Howe'er Philosophers dispute.

21 Ardelia to Melancholy

At last, my old inveterate foe,
No opposition shalt thou know.
Since I by struggling, can obtain
Nothing, but increase of pain,
I will att last, no more do soe,
Tho' I confesse, I have apply'd
Sweet mirth, and musick, and have try'd
A thousand other arts beside,
To drive thee from my darken'd breast,
Thou, who hast banish'd all my rest.
But, though sometimes, a short reprieve they gave,
Unable they, and far too weak, to save;
All arts to quell, did but augment thy force,
As rivers check'd, break with a wilder course.

Freindship, I to my heart have laid,
Freindship, th' applauded sov'rain aid,
And thought that charm so strong wou'd prove,
As to compell thee, to remove;
And to myself, I boastingly said,
Now I a conqu'rer sure shall be,
The end of all my conflicts, see,
And noble tryumph, wait on me;
My dusky, sullen foe, will sure
N'er this united charge endure.
But leaning on this reed, ev'n while I spoke
It peirc'd my hand, and into peices broke.
Still, some new object, or new int'rest came
And loos'd the bonds, and quite dissolv'd the claim.

These failing, I invok'd a Muse,
And Poetry wou'd often use,
To guard me from thy Tyrant pow'r;
And to oppose thee ev'ry hour
New troops of fancy's, did I chuse.

Alas! in vain, for all agree
To yeild me Captive up to thee
And heav'n, alone, can sett me free.
Thou, through my life, wilt with me goe,
And make yr passage, sad, and slow.
All, that cou'd ere thy ill gott rule, invade,
Their uselesse arms, before thy feet have laid;
The Fort is thine, now ruin'd, all within,
Whilst by decays without, thy Conquest too, is seen.

Ephelia: c. 1670

In his Anthology, *A Book of Women's Verse*, Sir John Squire asks: 'Who was Ephelia, first given her due in a charming essay by Mr. Gosse?'

22 Song

You wrong me, Strephon, when you say,
I'm jealous or severe,
Did I not see you kiss and play
With all you came annear?
Say, did I ever chide for this,
Or cast one jealous eye
On the bold nymphs, that snatch'd my bliss
While I stood wishing by.

Yet though I never disapproved
This modish liberty,
I thought in them you only loved
Change and variety:
I vainly thought my charms so strong,
And you so much my slave,
No nymph had power to do me wrong,
Or break the chains I gave.

But when you seriously address
With all your winning charms,
Unto a servile shepherdess,
I'll throw you from my arms:

I'd rather choose you should make love
  To every face you see,
Than Mopsa's dull admirer prove
  And let her rival me.

Elizabeth Rowe (Singer): 1674–1736

In 1710 she married Thomas Rowe, a miscellaneous author who was the son of a clergyman, and, according to Joyce Rowe (page 167), was a cousin of Elizabeth's contemporary, Nicholas Rowe, the poet-laureate. Mrs. Rowe's work was enthusiastically praised by Klopstock, Wieland and Dr. Samuel Johnson himself.

Johnson's praise may have been excited in part by the regularity of her 'numbers' and by the noble religious sentiment in her work—as exemplified by the poem which follows. An early commentator, referring to her light verse, never published, goes so far as to say, 'To a mind that had so entirely subdued its passions or devoted them to the honour of its Maker, and endued with the tenderest moral sense, what she could not absolutely approve, appeared unpardonable.'

23 God and His Creation

Ye woods and wilds, receive me to your shade!
These still retreats my contemplation aid:
From mortals flying to your chaste abode,
Let me attend th'instructing voice of God!
He speaks in all, and is in all things found;
I hear him, I perceive him all around;
In nature's lovely and unblemish'd face,
With joy his sacred lineaments I trace.
    O glorious Being! O supremely Fair!
How free, how perfect thy proportions are!
Forgive me, while with curious eyes I view
Thy works and boldly thus thy steps pursue:
The silent valley, and the lonely grove
I haunt: but Oh! 'tis thee I seek and love!
'Tis not the chant of birds, nor whispering breeze,
But thy soft voice I seek among the trees:

Invoking thee, by silver streams I walk,
To thee in solitary shades I talk:
I speak thy dear lov'd name, nor speak in vain;
Kind echoes long the pleasing sound retain.
Reviving sweets the op'ning flow'rs disclose,
Fragrant the violet, and the budding rose;
But all their balmy sweets from thee they steal,
And something of thee to my sense reveal.
Fair look the stars, and fair the morning ray,
When first the fields their painted scenes display;
Glorious the sun in his meridian height!
And yet, compar'd to thee, how faint the light!
Ador'd Artificer! What skill divine!
What wonders in the wide creation shine!
Order and majesty adorn the whole;
Beauty and life, and thou th' inspiring soul.
Whatever grace or harmony's express'd
On all thy works, the God is there confess'd:
But Oh, from all thy works, how small a part,
To human minds, is known of what thou art!
Fancy gives o'er its flight in search of thee:
Our thoughts are lost in thy immensity.

Mary Wortley Montagu (Pierrepont): 1689–1762

After reading the second of her poems in this book the reader will not be surprised to hear that she was an advocate of Women's Rights. It is for that reason that we have included those lines.

Her mother, a daughter of the Earl of Denbigh, died when Mary was a child. In 1712, despite the opposition of her father (Marquess of Dorchester and subsequently first Duke of Kingston), she eloped with Edward Wortley Montagu, scion of a family which came over with the Conqueror. In 1716 he was appointed ambassador to Turkey, and there the young people remained for two years. Lady Mary while living in Constantinople had the pluck to have her children inoculated against small-pox, and when she returned to England did her utmost, though vainly, to introduce the new-fangled notion. The best remembered of her writings is *Letters from the East*, of which an edition in the Everyman Library was published in 1906.

When she was fifty she left England; and although she never saw her husband again, they continued to correspond 'very civilly'. In late life she was gravely afflicted with a skin-disease to which Horace Walpole makes an unworthy reference. It was said to have disturbed her faculties at the end of her life.

24 In Answer to a Lady who Advised Retirement

You little know the heart that you advise;
I view this various scene with equal eyes:
In crowded courts I find myself alone,
And pay my worship to a nobler throne.
Long since the value of this world I know,
Pity the madness, and despise the show:
Well as I can my tedious part I bear,
And wait for my dismission without fear.
Seldom I mark mankind's detested ways,
Not hearing censure, nor affecting praise,
And, unconcern'd, my future state I trust
To that sole being, merciful and just.

25 A Caveat to the Fair Sex

Wife and servant are the same,
But only differ in the name;
For when the fatal knot is ty'd,
Which nothing, nothing can divide;
When she the word *obey* has said,
And man by law supreme is made,
Then all that's kind is laid aside,
And nothing left but state and pride:
Fierce as an Eastern prince he grows,
And all his innate rigour shows;
Then but to look, to laugh, to speak,
Will the nuptial contract break.

Like mutes, the signs alone must make,
And never any freedom take:
But still be govern'd by a nod,
And fear her husband as her god:
Him still must serve, him still obey,
And nothing act, and nothing say,
But what her haughty lord thinks fit,
Who with the power, has all the wit.
Then shun, O shun, that wretched state,
And all the fawning flatterers hate:
Value yourselves; and men despise,
You must be proud, if you'll be wise.

PART TWO

Part Two

THIS SECTION IS notable for the arrival of Scottish poets—Pagan, Blamire, Lindsay and Nairne: an effect, perhaps, of uniting the two kingdoms of England and Scotland. The Scots, as we now know, excelled the English, but the English poets are at least as robust as their male contemporaries.

The sentimentality which, coming in with Tom Moore, persisted in our literature for some sixty years (1820-1880) begins here with Mrs. Tighe and reaches its meridian with Mrs. Hemans, but we shall be unwise if we deride or ignore the prevailing mood of two generations.

If the contributors to this section are not highly distinguished, we must remember that, with the exception of Gray and Blake, the men-poets of the eighteenth century are now hardly read at all. The Age of Reason was naturally more successful in prose. In my judgement there are only three poems in Part Two that might have been written by men.

Marv Monk: ?–1715

She was the daughter of the first Viscount Molesworth of Swords, and married a gentleman who at one time was M.P. for Dublin. Her collected poems were published in the year after her death, an incident that seems somewhat ironically to have befallen several of our poets.

The following couplets will impress most readers by their sincerity and high courage.

26 Lines wirtten on her Death-bed

Thou, who dost all my worldly thoughts employ,
Thou pleasing source of all my earthly joy,
Thou tenderest husband and thou dearest friend,
To thee this first, this last, adieu I send.
At length, the conqueror death asserts his right,
And will for ever veil me from thy sight;

He woos me to him with a cheerful grace,
And not one terror clouds his meagre face:
He promises a lasting rest from pain,
And shows that all life's fleeting joys are vain:
The eternal scenes of heaven he sets in view,
And tells me that no other joys are true.
But love, fond love, would yet resist his power,
Would fain awhile defer the parting hour.
He brings thy mourning image to my eyes,
And would obstruct my journey to the skies.
But say, thou dearest, thou unwearied friend,
Say, should'st thou grieve to see my sorrow end?
Thou know'st a painful pilgrimage I've passed,
And should'st thou grieve that rest is come at last?
Rather rejoice to see me shake off life,
And die, as I have lived, thy faithful wife!

Mary Leapor: 1722–1746

She was a domestic servant, who died of measles at the age of 24, after teaching herself to read and write. Mary Leapor looked at Nature 'directly and keenly. A mere list of things she mentions (date 1746) astonishes the reader, accustomed, in the minor poet, to nothing more than groves, enamelled meads, bursting grapes, roses and lilies. If you turn her pages you will find kingcups, goldfinches, linnets, thyme, shining cottage tables, primroses, damsons, poppie.s' The quotation comes from Sir John Squire in *A Book of Women's Verse*. At this period 'spoiled' was pronounced 'spiled'.

27 Upon her Play being returned to her stained with Claret

Welcome, dear Wanderer, once more!
  Thrice welcome to thy native cell!
Within this peaceful humble door
  Let thou and I contented dwell!

But say, O whither hast thou rang'd?
  Why dost thou blush a crimson hue?
Thy fair complexion's greatly chang'd:
  Why, I can scarce believe 'tis you.

Then tell, my son, O tell me, where
  Didst thou contract this sottish dye?
You kept ill company, I fear,
  When distant from your parent's eye.

Was it for this, O graceless child,
  Was it for this you learn'd to spell?
Thy face and credit both are spoil'd;
  Go drown thyself in yonder well.

I wonder how thy time was spent:
  No news (Alas) hast thou to bring?
Hast thou not climb'd the Monument?
  Nor seen the lions, nor the King?

But now I'll keep you here secure:
  No more you view the smoky sky:
The court was never made (I'm sure)
  For idiots, like thee and I.

Isabel Pagan: 1740–1821

If a writer knew that after reaching the age of eighty-one she would be described by the *Dictionary of National Biography* as 'versifier', she might be somewhat depressed. The same authority states that 'she was credited by legend' with the song 'Ca' the yowes to the knowes' which continues, in Burns's version:

'Ca' them whare the heather grows,
Ca' them whare the burnie rowes,
My bonny dearie. . . .'

A yowe means an ewe; knowes are small hillocks. The lines that follow will get their true value if we imagine them sung to an old lilting tune at a crowded Fair.

28 The Answer

My Johnny is left me and gone to the sea,
I mourn for the absence of his company,
My parents was rich, and they did him despise,
And they advised me to do so likewise.

Alas! he has gone the wide world to range,
And were he but here now, my mind would soon change,
For sleeping and waking, I'm never at rest;
To think on my Johnny, my mind's sore oppress'd.

My love he is handsome in every degree,
Good natur'd and sober was his company,
He is voiced like a blackbird and eyed like a dove,
He is every way handsome, the man that I love.

And dearly I lov'd him, as I lov'd my life,
Although 'tis decreed that I'm not his wife;
Yet he has my heart in his bosom secure;
We are all born to troubles, I must that endure.

Anna Laetitia Barbauld (Aikin): 1743–1825

The next four poems are, as the reader may note, by one of the long-lived poets. In the happy lines to Mr. Barbauld (a presbyterian minister who came of a French protestant family) we see that rare poetic-bird, a tribute to domestic contentment; and the verses about flowers

'Gay without toil and lovely without art',

are already halfway rid of eighteenth-century stiffness. 'The Rights of Women' cannot justly be termed a poem, but in the present book it has an obvious interest. The last of the four, 'Life', is alike her best poem and the best-known. It is said to have been written when the author was eighty. Technically and in its sound this fine piece benefits immensely by the introduction of short lines refreshing to the ear.

The poet married in 1774.

29 To Mr. Barbauld

November 14, 1778

Come, clear thy studious looks awhile,
  'Tis arrant treason now
  To wear that moping brow,
When I, thy empress, bid thee smile.

What though the fading year
One wreath will not afford
To grace the poet's hair,
Or deck the festal board;

A thousand pretty ways we'll find
To mock old Winter's starving reign;
We'll bid the violets spring again,
Bid rich poetic roses blow,
Peeping above his heaps of snow;
We'll dress his withered cheeks in flowers,
  And on his smooth bald head
  Fantastic garlands bind:
  Garlands which we will get
From the gay blooms of that immortal year,
  Above the turning seasons set,
Where young ideas shoot in Fancy's sunny bowers.

  A thousand pleasant arts we'll have
To add new feathers to the wings of Time,
  And make him smoothly haste away:
  We'll use him as our slave,
And when we please we'll bid him stay,
And clip his wings, and make him stop to view
  Our studies, and our follies too;
How sweet our follies are, how high our fancies climb.

We'll little care what others do,
And where they go and what they say;
Our bliss, all inward and our own,
Would only tarnished be, by being shown.

The talking restless world shall see,
Spite of the world we'll happy be;
  But none shall know
  How much we're so,
Save only Love, and we.

30 To A Lady

with some painted flowers

. . . tibi lilia plenis
Ecce ferunt nymphæ calathis.
VIRGIL

Flowers to the fair: To you these flowers I bring,
And strive to greet you with an earlier spring.

Flowers, sweet and gay, and delicate like you,
Emblems of innocence and beauty too.
With flowers the Graces bind their yellow hair,
And flowery wreaths consenting lovers wear.
Flowers, the sole luxury which Nature knew,
In Eden's pure and guiltless garden grew.
To loftier forms are rougher tasks assigned;
The sheltering oak resists the stormy wind,
The tougher yew repels invading foes,
And the tall pine for future navies grows;
But this soft family, to cares unknown,
Were born for pleasure and delight alone:
Gay without toil, and lovely without art,
They spring to cheer the sense, and glad the heart.
Nor blush, my fair, to own you copy these,
Your best, your sweetest empire is—to please.

31 The Rights of Women

Yes, injured Woman! rise, assert thy right!
Woman! too long degraded, scorned, opprest;
O born to rule in partial Law's despite,
Resume thy native empire o'er the breast!

Go forth arrayed in panoply divine;
That angel pureness which admits no stain;
Go, bid proud Man his boasted rule resign,
And kiss the golden sceptre of thy reign.

Go, gird thyself with grace; collect thy store
Of bright artillery glancing from afar;
Soft melting tones thy thundering cannon's roar,
Blushes and fears thy magazine of war.

Thy rights are empire: urge no meaner claim,—
Felt, not defiled, and if debated, lost;
Like sacred mysteries, which withheld from fame,
Shunning discussion, are revered the most.

Try all that wit and art suggest to bend
Of thy imperial foe the stubborn knee;
Make treacherous Man thy subject, not thy friend;
Thou mayst command, but never canst be free.

Awe the licentious, and restrain the rude;
Soften the sullen, clear the cloudy brow:
Be, more than princes' gifts, thy favours sued;—
She hazards all, who will the least allow.

But hope not, courted idol of mankind,
On this proud eminence secure to stay;
Subduing and subdued, thou soon shalt find
Thy coldness soften, and thy pride give way.

Then, then, abandon each ambitious thought,
Conquest or rule thy heart shall feebly move,
In Nature's school, by her soft maxims taught,
That separate rights are lost in mutual love.

32 Life

Life! I know not what thou art,
But know that thou and I must part;
And when, or how, or where we met,
I own to me's a secret yet.
But this I know, when thou art fled,
Where'er they lay these limbs, this head,
No clod so valueless shall be
As all that then remains of me.

O whither, whither dost thou fly?
Where bend unseen thy trackless course?
And in this strange divorce,
Ah, tell where I must seek this compound I?
To the vast ocean of empyreal flame
From whence thy essence came
Dost thou thy flight pursue, when freed
From matter's base encumbering weed?
Or dost thou, hid from sight,
Wait, like some spell-bound knight,
Through blank oblivious years th' appointed hour
To break thy trance and reassume thy power?
Yet canst thou without thought or feeling be?
O say, what art thou, when no more thou'rt thee?

Life! we have been long together,
Through pleasant and through cloudy weather;
'Tis hard to part when friends are dear;
Perhaps 'twill cost a sigh, a tear;—
Then steal away, give little warning,
Choose thine own time;
Say not Good-night, but in some brighter clime
Bid me Good-morning.

Susanna Blamire: 1747–1794

She was called 'the Muse of Cumberland', her father having been a yeoman of that county; and it was in farming society that she spent most of her life. She wrote some of her poems in collaboration with her great friend Catherine Gilpin. Everybody agreed that Susanna Blamire had a happy and good-humoured personality.

33 The Siller Croun

And ye shall walk in silk attire,
  And siller hae to spare,
Gin ye'll consent to be his bride,
  Nor think o' Donald mair.
O wha wad buy a silken goun
  Wi' a poor broken heart!
Or what's to me a siller croun
  Gin frae my love I part!

The mind wha's every wish is pure
  Far dearer is to me;
And ere I'm forced to break my faith
  I'll lay me doun an' dee.
For I hae pledg'd my virgin troth
  Brave Donald's fate to share;
And he has gi'en to me his heart,
  Wi' a' its virtues rare.

His gentle manners wan my heart,
  He gratefu' took the gift;
Could I but think to seek it back
  It wad be waur than theft!
For langest life can ne'er repay
  The love he bears to me;
And ere I'm forced to break my troth
  I'll lay me doun an' dee.

Lady Sophia Burrell: 1750?–1802

Lady Burrell seems now to be an irrecoverable ghost—but a gay ghost. These quips will at least show one aspect of feminine humour and satire: so highly developed by some women-writers in our own day.

34 Epigram on Two Ladies

Which is the best to hit your taste,
Fat pork or scrag of mutton?
The last wou'd suit an invalid,
The first wou'd gorge a glutton.

If fat and plenty is your aim,
Let Phillis be your treat;
If leaner viands are your choice,
You Pamela may eat.

35 To Emma

Why, pretty rogue! do you protest
The trick of stealing you detest?
'Tis what you are doing ev'ry day,
Either in earnest or in play;
Cupid and you, 'tis said, are cousins,
(*Au fait* in stealing hearts by dozens,)
Who make no more of shooting 'sparks',
Than school-boys do of wounding larks;
Nay, what is worse, 'tis my belief,
Tho' known to be an arrant thief,
Such powers of witchcraft are your own,
That justice slumbers on her throne;
And shou'd you be arraign'd in court
For practising this cruel sport,
In spite of all the plaintiff's fury,
Your SMILE wou'd bribe both JUDGE and JURY.

Lady Anne Lindsay, later Lady Anne Barnard: 1750–1825

A daughter of the fifth Earl of Balcarres. She spent five years at the Cape of Good Hope with her husband and, when she returned to London, set up a literary salon in a house in Berkeley Square.

Somewhat mysteriously she would not acknowledge her authorship of 'Auld Robin Gray' until two years before her death, and then she confided the secret to Sir Walter Scott.

36 Auld Robin Gray

When the sheep are in the fauld, and the kye at hame,
And a' the warld to rest are gane,
The waes o' my heart fa' in showers frae my e'e,
When my gudeman lies sound by me.

Young Jamie loe'd me weel, and socht me for his bride,
But saving a crown, he had naething else beside;
To mak that crown a pund my Jamie gaed to sea,
And the crown and the pund were baith for me.

He hadna been awa a week but only twa,
When mother she fell sick, and the cow was stown awa,
My father brake his arm, and young Jamie at the sea,
And auld Robin Gray cam a courtin' me.

My father couldna work, and my mother couldna spin;
I toiled day and nicht, but their bread I couldna win,
Auld Rob maintained them baith, and wi' tears in his e'e,
Said 'Jenny, for their sake, oh, marry me!'

My heart it said Nay, for I looked for Jamie back,
But the wind it blew high, and the ship it was a wrack;
The ship it was a wrack—why didna Jamie dee?
Or why do I live to say 'Wae's me'!

My father argued sair, my mother didna speak,
But she lookit in my face till my heart was like to break,
Sae they gied him my hand, though my heart was in the sea,
And auld Robin Gray was gudeman to me.

I hadna been a wife a week but only four,
When sitting mournfully on the stane at the door,
I saw my Jamie's wraith, for I couldna think it he,
Till he said 'I've come back for to marry thee'.

Oh, sair did we greet and muckle did we say,
We took but ae kiss, and we tore ourselves away,
I wish I were dead, but I'm no like to dee,
And why do I live to say 'Wae's me'.?

I gang like a ghaist, and I carena to spin,
I daurna think on Jamie, for that wad be a sin,
But I'll do my best a gude wife to be,
For auld Robin Gray is kind unto me.

Fanny Greville: c. 1750

'The identity of Fanny Greville, whose *Indifference* is one of the most poignant lyrics of the eighteenth century, has always baffled historians.' We quote from Sir John Squire.

37 Prayer for Indifference

I ask no kind return in love,
  No tempting charm to please;
Far from the heart such gifts remove,
  That sighs for peace and ease.

Nor ease, nor peace, that heart can know,
  That, like the needle true,
Turns at the touch of joy or woe;
  But, turning, trembles too.

Far as distress the soul can wound
  'Tis pain in each degree;
'Tis bliss but to a certain bound,
  Beyond—is agony.

Joanna Baillie: 1762–1851

She was principally a writer of plays: 'Plays on the Passions' she called them: and the chief character in each play represented one of 'the Passions'. This approach to the drama, esteemed in her youth, long since rendered her dramatic work unreadable and unactable.

JOANNA BAILLIE

Born at Bothwell, on the banks of the Clyde, she was educated in Glasgow. In early days however she and her sister settled in Hampstead and there they remained for the rest of their lives—and Joanna Baillie's is our top score in longevity. When she was in her early fifties and a writer of high reputation, she seems to have missed her opportunity of meeting those youngsters Keats and Shelley who at that time were often in Hampstead.

Fortunately we have an admirable letter about her, written at Hampstead by a Miss E. Trevenen of Helston in Cornwall. The letter is dated 1833—when the poet-dramatist was seventy. The writer says: 'Our great poetess, or rather the sensible, amiable old lady that *was* a great poetess thirty years ago, is still in full preservation, as to health. Never did the flame of genius more thoroughly expire than in her case; for though, as Lamb says, "Ancient Mariners", "Lyrical Ballads", and "Kehamas" are not written in the grand clamacteric, the authors of such flights of imagination generally give out sparkles of their ancient fires in conversation; but Mrs. Joanna Baillie is, as Mr. Wordsworth observes, when quoting her non-feeling for Lycidas, "dry and Scotchy": learning she *never* possessed, and some of her poetry, which I think was far above that of any other woman, is the worse for a few specks of bad English; then her criticisms are so surprisingly narrow and jejune, and show so slight an acquaintance with fine literature in general. Yet if the authoress of "Plays on the Passions" does not now write or talk like a poetess, she *looks* like one, and *is* a piece of poetry in herself. Never was old age more lovely or interesting; the face, the dress, the quiet, subdued motions, the silver hair, the calm *in-looking* eye, the pale yet not unhealthy-looking skin, all are in harmony; this is winter with its own peculiar loveliness of snows and paler sunshine; no forced flowers or fruits to form an unnatural contrast with the general air of the prospect.'

Patriotic verse is now out of favour, but those who shrink from the sentiment of these simple robust verses should know that they were written (not published) in 1805, when the Napoleonic scare was at its height. 'Spear', even at this date, must have been a poeticism and a mere rhyme-word.

38 A Volunteer Song

Ye, who Britain's soldiers be,
Freemen, children of the free,
Who freely come at danger's call
From shop and palace, cot and hall,
And brace ye bravely up in warlike gear
For all that ye hold dear!

Blest in your hands be sword and spear!
There is no banded Briton here
On whom some fond mate hath not smil'd,
Or hung in love some lisping child;
Or aged parent, grasping his last stay
With looks of honour'd grey.

Such men behold with steady pride
The threaten'd tempest gath'ring wide,
And list, with onward forms inclin'd,
To sound of foemen on the wind,
And bravely act, 'mid the wild battle's roar,
In scenes untried before.

Let vet'rans boast, as well they may,
Nerves steel'd in many a bloody day;
The gen'rous heart, who takes his stand
Upon his free and native land,
Doth with the first sound of the hostile drum
A fearless man become.

Come then, ye hosts that madly pour
From wave-toss'd floats upon our shore!
If fell or gentle, false or true,
Let those enquire who wish to sue:
Nor fiend nor hero from a foreign strand,
Shall lord it in our land.

Come then, ye hosts that madly pour
From wave-toss'd floats upon our shore!
An adverse wind or breezeless main,
Lock'd in their ports our tars detain,
To waste their wishful spirits, vainly keen,
Else here ye had not been.

Yet, ne'ertheless, in strong array,
Prepare ye for a well-fought day,
Let banners wave, and trumpets sound,
And closing cohorts darken round,
And the fierce onset raise its mingled roar,
New sound on England's shore!

Freemen, children of the free,
Are brave alike on land or sea;
And every rood of English ground,
On which a hostile glove is found,
Proves, under their firm tread and vig'rous stroke,
A deck of royal oak.

39 The Kitten

Wanton drole, whose harmless play
Beguiles the rustic's closing day,
When drawn the evening fire about,
Sit aged crone and thoughtless lout,
And child upon his three-foot stool,
Waiting until his supper cool,
And maid, whose cheek outblooms the rose,
As bright the blazing faggot glows,
Who, bending to the friendly light,
Plies her task with busy sleight;
Come, show thy tricks and sportive graces,
Thus circled round with merry faces!
Backward coil'd, and crouching low,
With glaring eyeballs watch thy foe,
The housewife's spindle whirling round,
Or thread, or straw, that on the ground

Its shadow throws, by urchin sly
Held out to lure thy roving eye;
Then, onward stealing, fiercely spring
Upon the futile, faithless thing.
Now, wheeling round, with bootless skill,
Thy bo-peep tail provokes thee still,
As oft beyond thy curving side
Its jetty tip is seen to glide;
Till, from thy centre starting far,
Thou sidelong veer'st, with rump in air,
Erected stiff, and gait awry.
Like madam in her tantrums high:
Tho' ne'er a madam of them all
Whose silken kirtle sweeps the hall,
More varied trick and whim displays,
To catch the admiring stranger's gaze.
Doth power in varied measures dwell,
All thy vagaries wild to tell?
Ah no! the start, the jet, the bound,
The giddy scamper round and round,
With leap, and jerk, and high curvet,
And many a whirling somerset,
(Permitted by the modern muse
Expression technical to use.)
These mock the deftest rhymers skill,
But poor in art, tho' rich in will.
The featest tumbler, stage bedight,
To thee is but a clumsy wight,
Who every limb and sinew strains,
To do what costs thee little pains;
For which, I trow, the gaping crowd
Requites him oft with plaudits loud.
But, stopp'd the while thy wanton play,
Applauses too *thy* feats repay:
For then, beneath some urchin's hand,
With modest pride thou tak'st thy stand,
While many a stroke of fondness glides
Along thy back and tabby sides.

Dilated swells thy glossy fur,
And loudly sings thy busy purr;
As, timing well the equal sound,
Thy clutching feet bepat the ground,
And all their harmless claws disclose,
Like prickles of an early rose;
While softly from thy whisper'd cheek,
Thy half-clos'd eyes peer, mild and meek.

But not alone by cottage fire
Do rustics rude thy feats admire;
The learned sage, whose thoughts explore
The widest range of human lore,
Or, with unfetter'd fancy, fly
Thro' airy heights of poesy,
Pausing, smiles with alter'd air,
To see thee climb his elbow-chair,
Or, struggling on the mat below,
Hold warfare with his slipper'd toe.
The widow'd dame, or lonely maid,
Who in the still but cheerless shade
Of home unsocial, spends her age,
And rarely turns a letter'd page,
Upon her hearth for thee lets fall
The rounded cork, or paper ball,
Nor chides thee on thy wicked watch
The ends of ravell'd skein to catch,
But lets thee have thy wayward will,
Perplexing oft her sober skill.
E'en he, whose mind of gloomy bent,
In lonely tower or prison pent,
Reviews the coil of former days,
And loathes the world and all its ways;
What time the lamp's unsteady gleam,
Doth rouse him from his moody dream.
Feels, as thou gambol'st round his seat,
His heart with pride less fiercely beat,
And smiles, a link in thee to find
That joins him still to living kind.

Whence hast thou, then, thou witless puss,
The magic power to charm us thus?
Is it, that in thy glaring eye,
And rapid movements, we descry,—
While we at ease, secure from ill,
The chimney corner snugly fill,—
A lion darting on his prey,
A tiger at his ruthless play?
Or is it, that in thee we trace,
With all thy varied wanton grace,
An emblem viewed with kindred eye,
Of tricky, restless infancy?
Ah! many a lightly sportive child,
Who hath, like thee, our wit beguil'd,
To dull and sober mankind grown,
With strange recoil our hearts disown.
Even so, poor Kit! must thou endure,
When thou becom'st a cat demure,
Full many a cuff and angry word,
Chid roughly from the tempting board.
And yet, for that thou hast, I ween,
So oft our favour'd playmate been.
Soft be the change which thou shalt prove
When time hath spoil'd thee of our love;
Still be thou deem'd, by housewife fat,
A comely, careful mousing cat,
Whose dish is, for the public good,
Replenish'd oft with savoury food.
Nor when thy span of life is past,
Be thou to pond or dunghill cast;
But gently borne on goodman's spade,
Beneath the decent sod be laid,
And children show, with glistening eyes,
The place where poor old Pussy lies.

Carolina Oliphant, Baroness Nairne: 1766–1845

Only Shakespeare, Burns and Carolina Oliphant could claim that they wrote so many as three lyrics which after a hundred years or more are still known to everybody, for beside the two following, she wrote 'Caller Herring'. This poet was born at Gask, Perthshire, and it was there that she died. During her lifetime she wrote under the disguise of 'B.B.'—Mrs. Bogan of Bogan: and, once again, we find that a poet's work was collected and published in the year after her death. The book was called *Lays from Strathearn*. Her father was an ardent Jacobite, and she was named Carolina in memory of 'Bonnie Prince Charlie'.

When she married, she was forty. Her husband inherited the Barony (which had been created in 1681) when she was fifty-eight. After his death in 1830, she lived in County Wicklow and also travelled extensively in Europe.

40 Charlie is my Darling

'Twas on a Monday morning,
Right early in the year,
When Charlie came to our toun,
The young Chevalier.

Oh, Charlie is my darling,
My darling, my darling;
Oh, Charlie is my darling,
The young Chevalier.

As he came marching up the street,
The pipes play'd loud and clear,
And a' the folk came running out
To meet the Chevalier.

Oh, Charlie is my darling. . . .

Wi' Hieland bonnets on their heads,
And claymores bright and clear,
They came to fight for Scotland's right,
And the young Chevalier.

Oh, Charlie is my darling. . . .

They've left their bonnie Hieland hills,
  Their wives and bairnies dear,
To draw the sword for Scotland's lord,
  The young Chevalier.

Oh, Charlie is my darling. . . .

Oh, there were mony beating hearts,
  And mony a hope and fear,
And mony were the prayers put up
  For the young Chevalier.

Oh, Charlie is my darling,
  My darling, my darling;
Oh, Charlie is my darling,
  The young Chevalier.

41 Will ye no come back again?

Bonnie Charlie's now awa,
  Safely owre the friendly main;
Mony a heart will break in twa,
  Should he ne'er come back again.

Will ye no come back again?
Will ye no come back again?
Better lo'ed ye canna be,
Will ye no come back again?

Ye trusted in your Hieland men,
  They trusted you, dear Charlie;
They kent you hiding in the glen,
  Your cleadin was but barely.

Will ye no . . .

English bribes were a' in vain,
  An' e'en tho' puirer we may be;
Siller canna buy the heart
  That beats aye for thine and thee.

Will ye no . . .

We watched thee in the gloaming hour,
  We watched thee in the morning grey;
Tho' thirty thousand pounds they'd gie,
  Oh there is nane that wad betray.

Will ye no . . .

Sweet's the laverock's note and lang,
  Lilting wildly up the glen;
But aye to me he sings ae sang,
  Will ye no come back again?

Will ye no come back again?
Will ye no come back again?
Better lo'ed ye canna be,
Will ye no come back again?

Anna Maria Porter: (no dates)

We have taken the following hymn from an anthology compiled by Joanna Baillie and published in 1823. The poem is interesting on account of its difficult rhyme-scheme, and although some of its phrasing is old-fashioned it is in itself a notable projection of creative force.

42 Hymn on the Seasons

Now, when the kindling Spring breathes life and joy
  Through earth and air, perfuming field and bow'r;
While rings from every copse glad minstrelsy;
  And sparkling myriads float round shrub and flow'r;
While, flashing brightness, runs the river by,
  Or darkling dimples with morn's transient show'r,
(As shines thro' scattering clouds the azure sky,
  And laughs the golden sun in youthful pow'r;)
Now while all nature wakes, be my cheer'd eye
Rais'd joyous with my heart, to Him that dwells on high.

Father ador'd! O, let me still behold
  In these thy bounties, but thyself benign!
Still let me trace, in this terrestrial mould,
  The faint impression of that world divine,
Where all thy glory, wondrously unroll'd,
  Doth in the eyes of them for ever shine
Whom sin and death no more in fetters hold:
  O, let my earth-ward thoughts, with low decline,
No longer sink in languors dead and cold,
But spring with eager love thy footstool to enfold!

Give me, when song and fragrance round me flow,
  When blossoms show'r above, and ev'ry spray
Glitters with fost'ring dews; when the bright bow
  With colours jocund marks the chequer'd day;
When the freed birds their winter cells forego:
  And the lone cuchoo to morn's glimm'ring ray
Repeats his welcome strange; when bleat and low,
  Mingle with labour's voice and childhood's lay;
O not alone with pleasure let me glow,
But grateful join my song to all that hymn below!

Give me, when Summer's universal blush
  Spreads o'er the scene; when the broad woods expand
In screen umbrageous, and bank, and bush
  Are hung with roseate wreaths, by zephyr fann'd;
When panting heat lists to the cooling gush
  Of gelid springs, or marks the sportive band
Of skimming swallows o'er the gray lake rush;
  When sunny fruitage wooes each gath'ring hand,
And all mature the year; O, let the flush
Of raptur'd joy be mine, nor aught its transports hush!

And when clear ev'ning's star, with trembling beam
  Or sacred moonlight, thro' autumnal wood
Its lustre pours; when rock and valley gleam
  In shadowy distance, and no sounds intrude,
Save far-off village bells, or noiseless stream,
  Soothing the trance of heav'n-rapt solitude;

When paths, leaf-strewn, invite fond man to dream
  On the brief race of pleasure's insect brood;
Still of my musings lone be Thou the theme,
Nor aught thy wisdom scorns, let me momentous deem.

And when still Winter's breath the world congeals;
  When darken'd skies look mournful on the plain,
Where gath'ring ice o'er rushy shallows steals;
  When transient thaw descends in plashy rain,
Or sudden hail the cold blue heav'n reveals;
  When shiv'ring red-breasts join the household train,
And the rough ass no more his scanty meals
  Finds 'mid the snow-spread waste, or desert lane,
E'en then when nature's eye thy mercy seals,
O, be mine fix'd on all that death-like sleep conceals.

Miss Holford: (no dates)

This lady (she would not have resented the word) is another of Joanna Baillie's flock, and we cannot discover even her Christian name. The student may sense the influence of Byron upon the style of the poem, though not in its royalist sentiment. Here again we have a small work of high technical achievement, a poem strong in substance and in phrasing. Let us take it sincerely to our 'careless bosoms'. . . .

43 Lines

Suggested by a portrait of the unfortunate Queen of France, taken on the last examination previous to execution

And this was she! the peerless and the bright,
  The false world's darling! she who did possess,
(And held awhile in Europe's dazzled sight,)
  Glorious in majesty and loveliness,
  The Heaven-lent pow'r to ruin or to bless!
Yes,—this was she!—But mark ye, I beseech,
  Who love the world,—mark this mute wretchedness,
And grave it on your hearts, for it doth reach
To regions unexplor'd by eloquence of speech!

Nature gave loveliness, and fate gave pow'r,
  And millions lavished incense.—Poets hung
Their amaranth garlands o'er the royal bow'r;
  For Gallia's lily ev'ry lyre was strung,
  Pride of all eyes, and theme of ev'ry tongue:—
Love, awe, and wonder, were her ministers;
  Life, and its hours, upon her fiat hung;
She held in poise a nation's hopes and fears—
Dominion, beauty, pomp, and the world's shout, were hers!

Gracious and mighty! Yet there came an hour
  Of desolation; and away it swept,
In one rude whirlwind, empire, pomp, and pow'r!
  O'er the fair brow the hoary winter crept
  Of sorrow, not of time.—Those eyes have wept
Till grief had done with tears, and calm and cold,
  Tired with its own excess, in stupor slept,
Or gazed in frozen wonder to behold
The black and hideous page of destiny unroll'd.

Yet trace these faded lines! For they impart
  A tale, may do your careless bosoms good!
Muse o'er the fragments of a mighty heart,
  Broken by sorrow,—ye, whose jocund mood,
  Insatiate feeds on pleasure's tempting food:
Look here! It will not harm ye, tho' your thought
  Leave its gay flight to melt in pity's flood!
To each light heart, home be the lesson brought,
With what enduring bliss the world's fair smile is fraught!

And is this all? No; ye may learn beside,
  That *all* which fate can threaten *may* be borne;
To see life's blessings, one by one, subside,
  In its wild extremes from tenderness to scorn,
  But as the changes of an April morn!
For still she was a Queen! and majesty
  Surviv'd, tho' she, deserted and forlorn,
Save Heav'n, had ne'er a friend to lift her eye;
But Heav'n return'd the glance, and taught her how to die.

Mrs. J. Hunter: (no dates)

Joanna Baillie was evidently no prude or she would not have welcomed this dainty lyric about a wanton. We are left wondering how the rose-like Lelia, presumably a girl of the Regency, had sinned, but at least we know that she must early have left the path of righteousness —almost as soon, in fact, as she met 'the orb of day' or, in other words, was mature. On the other hand, she may be a fragment of Mrs. Hunter's 'subliminal consciousness'.

44 A Simile

I saw the wild rose on its parent thorn,
  Half clos'd, soft blushing, thro' the glitt'ring dew,
Wave on the breeze, and scent the breath of morn;
  Lelia, the lovely flow'r resembled you.

Scarce had it spread to meet the orb of day,
  Its fragrant beauties op'ning to the view,
When ruffian blasts have torn the rose away;
  Lelia—alas! it still resembles you!

So, torn, by wild and lawless passion's force,
  From every social tie, thy lot must be;
At best oblivion shades thy future course,
  And still the hapless flow'r resembles thee!

Mary Tighe (Blackford): 1772–1810

The reader may be surprised by the inclusion of a sonnet so mediocre, but it has the unusual interest of being by a writer who at one time influenced no less a poet than John Keats. Mary Tighe, who made an unhappy marriage with a cousin, was the daughter of an Irish clergyman; and it was in Kilkenny that she died. In 1805 (when Keats was ten years old) she published a fairly long poem in level melodious stanzas—*Psyche, or the Legend of Love*, based on the classical romance by Apuleius. The *Quarterly Review*, afterwards 'so savage and tartarly' towards Keats, praised the poem. A contemporary critic, in a somewhat beaver-hatted style, wrote of her 'To possess strong feelings and amiable affections, and to express them with a nice discrimination, has been the attribute of many female writers; some of whom have also participated with the author of *Psyche* in the unhappy lot of a suffering frame and a premature death.'

Everyone knows that as a poet, Keats, like Shelley, started badly. In his 1817 volume he published a deplorable set of verses 'To some ladies'. They contain the lines:

> And now! ah, I see it—you just now are stooping
> To pick up the keepsake intended for me.
>
> If a cherub, on pinions of silver descending,
> Had brought me a gem from the fret-work of heaven;
> And smiles, with his star-cheering voice sweetly blending,
> The blessings of Tighe had melodiously given. . . .

A year and a half later, Keats, whose development may have been quickened by tuberculosis, had perceived his mistake. He says in a letter:

> 'Mrs. Tighe and Beattie once delighted me—now I see through them and can find nothing in them or weakness, and yet how many they still delight! Perhaps a superior being may look upon Shakespeare in the same light—is it possible? No . . .'

45 Sonnet

As one who late hath lost a friend adored,
Clings with sick pleasure to the faintest trace
Resemblance offers in another's face,
Or sadly gazing on that form deplored,
Would clasp the silent canvass to his breast:
So muse I on the good I have enjoyed,
The wretched victim of my hope destroyed;
On images of peace I fondly rest,
Or on the page, where weeping fancy mourns,

I love to dwell upon each tender line,
And think the bliss once tasted still is mine;
While cheated memory to the past returns,
And, from the present, leads my shivering heart
Back to those scenes from which it wept to part.

Caroline Southey (Bowles): 1787–1854

Being in money difficulties, Caroline Bowles in 1820 sent her poem 'Ellen Fitzarthur' to the well-established poet Robert Southey. Nineteen years later she became his second wife—when she was fifty-three.

In 1852 Queen Victoria gave her an annual pension of £200. Here is a poem which, if examined minutely, is a clear specimen of 'feminine poetry'. No man could have written, for example, the first three lines of the last verse.

46 To Death

Come not in terrors clad, to claim
An unresisting prey:
Come like an evening shadow, Death!
So stealthily, so silently!
And shut mine eyes, and steal my breath;
Then willingly, O willingly,
With thee I'll go away.

What need to clutch with iron grasp
What gentlest touch may take?
What need with aspect dark to scare,
So awfully, so terribly,
The weary soul would hardly care,
Call'd quietly, call'd tenderly,
From thy dread power to break?

'Tis not as when thou markest out
The young, the blest, the gay,
The loved, the loving—they who dream
So happily, so hopefully;
Then harsh thy kindest call may seem,
And shrinkingly, reluctantly,
The summon'd may obey.

But I have drunk enough of life—
The cup assign'd to me
Dash'd with a little sweet at best,
So scantily, so scantily—
To know full well that all the rest
More bitterly, more bitterly,
Drugg'd to the last will be.

And I may live to pain some heart
That kindly cares for me:
To pain, but not to bless. O Death!
Come quietly—come lovingly—
And shut mine eyes, and steal my breath;
Then willingly, O willingly,
I'll go away with thee!

Felicia Hemans (Browne): 1793–1835

With Mrs. Hemans we find ourselves in the Age of Sentimentality, but we should remember that the young Charles Dickens was also contributing to it. Felicia Browne was born in Liverpool. Her father was Irish, her mother Austrian. Her patriotic verse must have been stimulated by the fact that two of her brothers fought in Spain under Sir John Moore: but patriotism in her day was, of course, instinctive and almost universal.

She married at the age of nineteen, and she bore five sons. Six years after her marriage, Captain Hemans (an army man) went alone to Rome, and although Felicia and he never met again, they corresponded amiably. In 1827 her mother died, and the poet, developing heart trouble, was thereafter an invalid. She died in Dublin.

Sir Walter Scott criticised her verse as 'too poetical', and as having 'too many flowers, too little fruit'; but on parting from her, after she had stayed some time at Abbotsford, Sir Walter said, 'There are some whom we meet and should like ever after to claim as Kith and Kin; and you are one of those.'

Mrs. Hemans wrote the once-hackneyed ballad, 'The boy stood on the burning deck', in which she commemorated a moving example of youthful heroism. Her outlook and her style may now be as far outmoded as daguerreotypes, but we are shallow readers if we cannot imaginatively sympathise with bygone fashions and enthusiasms.

The 'hamlet fanes' are presumably village churches.

47 The Cliffs of Dover

'The inviolate Island of the sage and free.'

BYRON

Rocks of my country! let the cloud
Your crested heights array,
And rise ye like a fortress proud
Above the surge and spray!

My spirit greets you as ye stand,
Breasting the billow's foam:
Oh! thus for ever guard the land,
The severed land of home!

I have left rich blue skies behind,
Lighting up classic shrines,
And music in the southern wind,
And sunshine on the vines.

The breathings of the myrtle flowers
Have floated o'er my way;
The pilgrim's voice, at vesper hours,
Hath soothed me with its lay.

The isles of Greece, the hills of Spain,
The purple heavens of Rome—
Yes, all are glorious,—yet again
I bless thee, land of home!

For thine the Sabbath peace, my land!
And thine the guarded hearth;
And thine the dead—the noble band,
That make thee holy earth.

Their voices meet me in thy breeze,
  Their steps are on thy plains;
Their names, by old majestic trees,
  Are whispered round thy fanes.

Their blood hath mingled with the tide
  Of thine exulting sea:
Oh! be it still a joy, a pride,
  To live and die for thee.

48 The Homes of England

'Where's the coward that would not dare
  To fight for such a land?'
MARMION

The stately homes of England,
  How beautiful they stand,
Amidst their tall ancestral trees,
  O'er all the pleasant land!
The deer across their greensward bound,
  Through shade and sunny gleam;
And the swan glides past them with the sound
  Of some rejoicing stream.

The merry homes of England!
  Around their hearths by night,
What gladsome looks of household love
  Meet in the ruddy light!
There woman's voice flows forth in song,
  Or childhood's tale is told,
Or lips move tunefully along
  Some glorious page of old.

The blessèd homes of England!
  How softly on their bowers
Is laid the holy quietness
  That breathes from Sabbath hours!

Solemn, yet sweet, the church-bell's chime
  Floats through their woods at morn;
All other sounds, in that still time,
  Of breeze and leaf are born.

The cottage homes of England!
  By thousands on her plains,
They are smiling o'er the silvery brooks,
  And round the hamlet fanes.
Through glowing orchards forth they peep,
  Each from its nook of leaves;
And fearless there the lowly sleep,
  As the bird beneath their eaves.

The free, fair homes of England!
  Long, long, in hut and hall,
May hearts of native proof be reared
  To guard each hallowed wall!
And green for ever be the groves,
  And bright the flowery sod,
Where first the child's glad spirit loves
  Its country and its God!

Sara Coleridge: 1802–1850

This lady was born at Keswick, the only daughter of that wayward genius Samuel Taylor Coleridge. Brought up in the most intellectual atmosphere of the time, she learned to read Greek, Latin, French, German, Italian and Spanish. For seven years she was engaged to a barrister, one of her cousins, whom she married. With him she lived for eight years in a cottage at Hampstead, probably the part of London that is richest in literary associations. They then removed to Chester Place, Regent's Park.

She is celebrated in one of Wordsworth's flattest effusions, written in 1828. After praising Dora, his daughter, and Edith Southey, the poet says of Sara:

Her brow hath opened on me—see it there,
Brightening the umbrage of her hair;
So gleams the crescent moon, that loves
To be descried through shady groves.
Tenderest bloom is on her cheek;
Wish not for a richer streak. . . .

and so on. The last line clamours for inclusion in an anthology of 'worst lines'.

Her verses are in a faded mode, but in savouring poetry we should always extract the essential emotion out of the temporal vocabulary. 'Nook', 'kine' and 'fane' are not words which a living poet would use. They had emotional reality to Sara Coleridge.

49 I tremble when with looks benign . . .

I tremble when with looks benign
Thou tak'st my offer'd hand in thine,
Lest passion-breathing words of mine
The charm should break:
And friendly smiles be forced to fly,
Like soft reflections of the sky,
Which, when rude gales are sweeping by,
Desert the lake.

Of late I saw thee in a dream;
The day-star pour'd his hottest beam,
And thou, a cool refreshing stream,
Did'st brightly run.
The trees where thou wert pleased to flow,
Threw out their flowers, a glorious show,
While I, too distant doomed to grow,
Pined in the sun.

By no life-giving moisture fed,
A wasted tree, I bow'd my head,
My sallow leaves and blossoms shed
On earth's green breast:

And silent pray'd the slumbering wind,
The lake, thy tarrying place, might find,
And waft my leaves, with breathings kind,
There, there to rest.

50 I thought by tears...

I thought by tears thy soul to move
Since smiles had proved in vain;
But I from thee no smiles of love,
Nor tears of pity gain.
Now, now I could not smile perforce
A sceptred queen to please:
Yet tears will take th'accustom'd course
Till time their fountain freeze.

My life is dedicate to thee,
My service wholly thine;
But what fair fruit can grace the tree
Till suns vouchsafe to shine?
Thou art my sun, thy looks are light,
O cast me not in shade—
Beam forth ere summer takes its flight,
And all my honours fade.

When torn by sudden gusty flaw,
The fragile harp lies mute,
Its tenderest tones the wind can draw
From many another lute;
But when this beating heart lies still,
Each chord relax'd in death,
What other shall so deeply thrill,
So tremble at thy breath?

51 The Mother

Full oft beside some gorgeous fane
The youngling heifer bleeds and dies;
Her life-blood issuing forth amain,
While wreaths of incense climb the skies.

The mother wanders all around,
   Thro' shadowy grove and lightsome glade;
Her footmarks on the yielding ground
   Will prove what anxious quest she made.

The stall where late her darling lay
   She visits oft with eager look;
In restless movements wastes the day,
   And fills with cries each neighb'ring nook.

She roams along the willowy copse,
   Where purest waters softly gleam;
But ne'er a leaf or blade she crops,
   Nor couches by the gliding stream.

No youthful kine, tho' fresh and fair,
   Her vainly searching eyes engage;
No pleasant fields relieve her care,
   No murmuring streams her grief assuage.

PART THREE

Part Three

AS TIME PROCEEDS, women begin to write more and more confidently in a feminine mode. The reader is unlikely to judge that a single poem in this section of the book could have come from a man.

There is still a slightly old-fashioned air about these poems, and it is largely caused by the use of the now-discarded Second Person Singular—'thee' and 'thou'. The loss of this form is an impoverishment of our language, and it is presumably irrecoverable.

We have now come into a period of famous names—for example, Mrs. Browning, the Brontë sisters and Christina Rossetti.

Elizabeth Barrett Browning (Barrett): 1806–1861

The daughter of a prolific and tyrannical father, the poet early became a fine classical scholar. In her teens she had a fall from a horse and was afterwards encouraged in invalidism by her father so that she should not marry and leave the household. Her poetry was at once appreciated, Edgar Allan Poe being one of her most enthusiastic admirers; and when she fell in love with the poet Robert Browning, she was better known than he was. Owing to her father's attitude, the lovers had to elope. They married at Marylebone Church, and experienced their honeymoon in Italy, where indeed they spent the larger part of their married life. The noble and famous 'Sonnets from the Portuguese' were not read by Browning until his wife rather shyly gave them to him at Bagni di Lucca during their honeymoon in 1844.

Mrs. Browning is certainly a front-rank poet. Her verse-novel *Aurora Leigh* is the best long poem which had then been written in England since *Paradise Lost*. It was greatly admired by so independent a judge as Dante Gabriel Rossetti, and is likely to take in the future a much higher place in literary estimation than it occupies at present.

52 Sonnets from the Portuguese

XIII

And wilt thou have me fashion into speech
The love I bear thee, finding words enough,
And hold the torch out, while the winds are rough,
Between our faces, to cast light on each?—
I drop it at thy feet. I cannot teach
My hand to hold my spirit so far off
From myself—me—that I should bring thee proof
In words, of love hid in me out of reach.
Nay, let the silence of my womanhood
Commend my woman-love to thy belief.—
Seeing that I stand unwon, however wooed,
And rend the garment of my life, in brief,
By a most dauntless, voiceless fortitude,
Lest one touch of this heart convey its grief.

53 XIV

If thou must love me, let it be for nought
Except for love's sake only. Do not say
'I love her for her smile—her look—her way
Of speaking gently,—for a trick of thought
That falls in well with mine, and certes brought
A sense of pleasant ease on such a day'—
For these things in themselves, Belovèd, may
Be changed, or change for thee,—and love, so wrought,
May be unwrought so. Neither love me for
Thine own dear pity's wiping my cheeks dry,—
A creature might forget to weep, who bore
Thy comfort long, and lose thy love thereby!
But love me for love's sake, that evermore
Thou may'st love on, through love's eternity.

54 XV

Accuse me not, beseech thee, that I wear
Too calm and sad a face in front of thine;
For we two look two ways, and cannot shine
With the same sunlight on our brow and hair.
On me thou lookest with no doubting care,
As on a bee shut in a crystalline;
Since sorrow hath shut me safe in love's divine,
And to spread wing and fly in the outer air
Were most impossible failure, if I strove
To fail so. But I look on thee—on thee—
Beholding, besides love, the end of love,
Hearing oblivion beyond memory;
As one who sits and gazes from above,
Over the rivers to the bitter sea.

55 XXXVIII

First time he kissed me, he but only kissed
The fingers of this hand wherewith I write;
And ever since, it grew more clean and white,
Slow to world-greetings, quick with its 'Oh, list,'
When the angels speak. A ring of amethyst
I could not wear here plainer to my sight,
Than that first kiss. The second passed in height
The first, and sought the forehead, and half missed,
Half falling on the hair. O beyond meed!
That was the chrism of love, which love's own crown,
With sanctifying sweetness, did precede.
The third, upon my lips, was folded down
In perfect, purple state; since when, indeed,
I have been proud and said, 'My love, my own.'

56 XLIII

How do I love thee? Let me count the ways.
I love thee to the depth and breadth and height
My soul can reach, when feeling out of sight
For the ends of Being and ideal Grace.

I love thee to the level of every day's
Most quiet need, by sun and candlelight.
I love thee freely, as men strive for Right;
I love thee purely, as they turn from Praise.
I love thee with the passion put to use
In my old griefs, and with my childhood's faith.
I love thee with a love I seemed to lose
With my lost saints,—I love thee with the breath,
Smiles, tears, of all my life!—and, if God choose,
I shall but love thee better after death.

57 On a portrait of Wordsworth

by B. R. Haydon

Wordsworth upon Helvellyn! Let the cloud
Ebb audibly along the mountain-wind
Then break against the rock, and show behind
The lowland valleys floating up to crowd
The sense with beauty. He, with forehead bowed
And humble-lidded eyes, as one inclined
Before the sovran thought of his own mind,
And very meek with inspirations proud,—
Takes here his rightful place as poet-priest
By the high altar, singing prayer and prayer
To the higher Heavens. A noble vision free
Our Haydon's hand has flung out from the mist:
No portrait this, with Academic air—
This is the poet and his poetry.

Helena Selina, Lady Dufferin (Sheridan): 1807–1876

The reader should refer to the subsequent note on Caroline Norton, for here is her sister—she who said to Disraeli that she ought to be the good sister of 'The Three Graces' although (she declared) she was not. Her life was happier than Caroline's and she had by her first husband a son, that 'great gentleman' and able diplomatist, the Marquess of Dufferin and Ava. The Marquess built a tower in her honour. Both

Tennyson and Browning composed inscriptions for it, but neither poet did himself justice.

In 1862 she married the Earl of Gifford when he was on his deathbed.

58 To my dearest son

With a chain made from my hair
June 21, 1860

Great love doth keep a Royal state
In those true hearts wherein he reigns;
Laws, language, coinage, value, rate
Of meaner monarchs he disdains.

Love hath a language for all years—
Fond hieroglyphs, obscure and old—
Wherein the heart reads, writ in tears,
The tale that never yet was told.

Love hath his meter too, to trace
Those bounds which never yet were given,
To measure that which mocks at space,
Is deep as death, and high as heaven.

Love hath his treasure hoards, to pay
True faith, or goodly service done,—
Dear priceless nothings, which outweigh
All riches that the sun shines on.

And from that treasure house he brings
E'en such a gift, this morn, for thee—
The best of those poor precious things
He hoards within his treasury.

A slender chain and yet more sure
Than steel to bind, than gold to sway—
A fragile thing—that shall endure—
When life and love have passed away.

The Hon. Mrs. Caroline Norton (Sheridan): 1808–1876

This brilliant and beautiful person was the model for the heroine in George Meredith's novel *Diana of the Crossways*. She was one of three granddaughters, famous for their beauty, of Sheridan the playwright. Lady Dufferin, one of the trio, said to Disraeli, 'Georgy' (afterwards Duchess of Somerset) 'is the beauty, Carrie is the wit, and I ought to be the good one, but I'm not.'

Caroline Sheridan's life was heavily scarred by her marriage to the Hon. George Norton. After three years with him she left the house. Presently she tried again, and in 1836 the Hon. George brought a charge against her of misconduct with the chilly Lord Melbourne, Queen Victoria's Prime Minister, but the jury dismissed the case without leaving the box. Her husband then failed to pay her allowance and even claimed her literary royalties, presumably because at that time a woman's money belonged to her husband. This injustice caused the poet to write to Queen Victoria, not without effect, concerning divorce-reform and the legal status of women.

Mr. Norton died in 1875, and in the last year of her own life Caroline Norton married Sir William Stirling-Maxwell.

59 I would the world were mine

Oh! I would the world were all mine own,
With its gay green fields and its rosy bowers,
And its drooping trees, where I alone
Might gather the buds that first were blown,
And weave a thousand fairy bowers
For thee—for thee!

Oh! I would the world were mine, with all
Its changeful skies which the soft stars beam in!
No scorching rays of the sun should fall,
But it should be to me, to all,
A moonlight world for Love to dream in
Of thee—of thee.

Oh! I would the world were mine, for then
I'd still the waves of the boundless ocean,
And swiftly I'd fly from the haunts of men
In some fairy bark which returned again
The dark blue waters' rippling motion,
With thee—With thee.

Oh! would that the world indeed could be
All, all my own—'twould then be thine!
Thy heart were world enough for me,
And to gain it I'd give the earth and sea—
Oh! worlds on worlds, if they were mine—
To thee—to thee.

60 I do not love thee

I do not love thee! No! I do not love thee!
And yet when thou art absent I am sad;
And envy even the bright blue sky above thee,
Whose quiet stars may see thee and be glad.

I do not love thee! Yet, I know not why,
Whate'er thou dost seems still well done, to me—
And often in my solitude I sigh—
That those I *do* love are not more like thee!

I do not love thee! yet, when thou art gone
I hate the sound (though those who speak be dear)
Which breaks the lingering echo of the tone
Thy voice of music leaves upon my ear.

I do not love thee! yet thy speaking eyes,
With their deep, bright, and most expressive blue—
Between me and the midnight heaven arise,
Oftener than any eyes I ever knew.

I *know* I do not love thee! yet, Alas!
Others will scarcely trust my candid heart;
And oft I catch them smiling as they pass,
Because they see me gazing where thou art.

Frances Anne Kemble: 1809–1893

This writer is the famous Shakespearean actress, Fanny Kemble. She toured the United States with her father, Charles Kemble, in 1832-4, helping greatly to restore his fortunes: and here she met and married a Southern planter. They were divorced in 1849. Her poems were published in 1844.

61 Paola and Francesca

Seer of the triple realm invisible,
When I beheld that miserable twain,
By Rimini's sudden sword of justice slain,
Sweep through the howling hurricane of hell—
Light seems to me to rest upon their gloom,
More than upon this wretched earth above,
Falls on the path of many a living love,
Whose fate may envy their united doom.
There be, who wandering in this world, with heart
Riveted to some other heart for ever,
Past power of all eternity to sever,
The current of this life still drives apart,
Who, with strained eyes, and outstretched arms, and cry
Of bitterest longing, come each other nigh,
To look, to love, and to be swept asunder,
The breathless greeting of their agony
Lost in the pitiless world-storm's ceaseless thunder.

Charlotte Brontë: 1816–1855

The father of three famous women-writers came from Ireland, and he changed his name from Brunty or Prunty. Before going to Cambridge University, taking holy orders and settling down as vicar of Haworth in Yorkshire, he had been a weaver and a schoolmaster in his native land. His wife came from a Cornish family named Branwell and, somewhat pathetically, wrote a book called *The Advantages of Poverty in Religious Concerns*.

Charlotte Brontë became a schoolmistress in Dewsbury and, after rejecting two clerical offers of marriage, she took work as a nursery governess. In 1842 she went with her sister Emily to study at a school in Brussels. In 1844 Charlotte returned to the Yorkshire vicarage. In 1846 the three sisters published, unsuccessfully, *Poems by Currer, Ellis and Acton Bell*. Two copies were sold.

Five years later a Mr. Taylor, associated with her publishers, vainly proposed to her. In 1854 she accepted her father's curate and was married to him at Haworth Church. In March 1855 she died of 'an illness incidental to childbirth', perhaps puerperal fever?

Her life was written in 1857 by the celebrated Mrs. Gaskell.

62 Watching and Wishing

Oh, would I were the golden light
  That shines around thee now,
As slumber shades the spotless white
  Of that unclouded brow!
It watches through each changeful dream
  Thy features' varied play;
It meets thy waking eyes' soft gleam
  By dawn—by op'ning day.

Oh, would I were the crimson veil
  Above thy couch of snow,
To dye thy cheek so soft, so pale,
  With my reflected glow!
Oh, would I were the cord of gold
  Whose tassel set with pearls
Just meets the silken cov'ring's fold
  And rests upon thy curls,

Dishevell'd in thy rosy sleep,
  And shading soft thy dreams;
Across their bright and raven sweep
  The golden tassel gleams!
I would be anything for thee,
  My love—my radiant love—
A flower, a bird, for sympathy,
  A watchful star above.

Emily Brontë: 1818–1848

The *Encyclopaedia Britannica* (1911) says that this poet's 'Old Stoic' and 'Last Lines' are 'probably the finest achievement of poetry that any woman has given to English literature'. She is, of course, the author of that impressive novel, *Wuthering Heights.* She died at the vicarage in 1848.

63 Remembrance

Cold in the earth—and the deep snow piled above thee,
Far, far removed, cold in the dreary grave!
Have I forgot, my only Love, to love thee,
Severed at last by Time's all-severing wave?

Now, when alone, do my thoughts no longer hover
Over the mountains, on that northern shore,
Resting their wings where heath and fern-leaves cover
Thy noble heart for ever, ever more?

Cold in the earth—and fifteen wild Decembers,
From those brown hills, have melted into spring:
Faithful, indeed, is the spirit that remembers
After such years of change and suffering!

Sweet Love of youth, forgive, if I forget thee,
While the world's tide is bearing me along;
Other desires and other hopes beset me,
Hopes which obscure, but cannot do thee wrong!

No later light has lightened up my heaven,
No second morn has ever shone for me;
All my life's bliss from thy dear life was given,
All my life's bliss is in the grave with thee.

But, when the days of golden dreams had perished,
And even Despair was powerless to destroy;
Then did I learn how existence could be cherished,
Strengthened, and fed without the aid of joy.

Then did I check the tears of useless passion—
Weaned my young soul from yearning after thine;
Sternly denied its burning wish to hasten
Down to that tomb already more than mine.

And, even yet, I dare not let it languish,
Dare not indulge in memory's rapturous pain;
Once drinking deep of that divinest anguish,
How could I seek the empty world again.

64 No coward soul is mine

No coward soul is mine,
No trembler in the world's storm-troubled sphere:
I see Heaven's glories shine,
And faith shines equal, arming me from fear.

O God within my breast,
Almighty, ever-present Deity!
Life—that in me has rest,
As I—undying Life—have power in thee!

Vain are the thousand creeds
That move men's hearts: unutterably vain;
Worthless as withered weeds,
Or idlest froth amid the boundless main,

To waken doubt in one
Holding so fast by thine infinity;
So surely anchored on
The stedfast rock of immortality.

With wide-embracing love
Thy spirit animates eternal years,
Pervades and broods above,
Changes, sustains, dissolves, creates, and rears.

Though earth and man were gone,
And suns and universes ceased to be,
And Thou wert left alone,
Every existence would exist in Thee.

There is not room for Death,
Nor atom that his might could render void:
Thou—THOU art Being and Breath,
And what THOU art may never be destroyed.

'George Eliot' (Mary Ann Evans): 1819–1880

The famous novelist married a Mr. Cross of whom we hear little. Early in life she became a Positivist. In 1854 she made 'a lifelong union without legal form with George Henry Lewes', the philosopher and dramatic critic. Her poems appeared in 1869 and 1874. She is probably, to her loss, the least feminine of the poets in this collection.

65 *From:* The Spanish Gipsy

It was in the prime
Of the sweet Spring-time
In the linnet's throat
Trembled the love-note,
And the love-stirred air
Thrilled the blossoms there.
Little shadows danced
Each a tiny elf
Happy in large light
And the thinnest self.

It was but a minute
In a far-off Spring,
But each gentle thing,
Sweetly-wooing linnet,
Soft-thrilled hawthorn tree,

Happy shadowy elf
With the thinnest self,
Lives still on in me.
O, the sweet, sweet prime
Of the past Spring-time!

66 The Choir Invisible

Longum illud tempusquum non ero magis me movet
quam hoc exiguum.—CICERO, ad Att. xii. 18

O may I join the choir invisible
Of those immortal dead who live again
In minds made better by their presence: live
In pulses stirred to generosity,
In deeds of daring rectitude, in scorn
For miserable aims that end with self,
In thoughts sublime that pierce the night like stars,
And with their mild persistence urge man's search
To vaster issues.
So to live is heaven:
To make undying music in the world,
Breathing as beauteous order that controls
With growing sway the growing life of man.
So we inherit that sweet purity
For which we struggled, failed and agonized
With widening retrospect that bred despair.
Rebellious flesh that would not be subdued,
A vicious parent shaming still its child
Poor anxious penitence, is quick dissolved;
Its discords, quenched by meeting harmonies,
Die in the large and charitable air.
And all our rarer, better, truer self,
That sobb'd religiously in yearning song,
That watch'd to ease the burthen of the world,
Laboriously tracing what must be,
And what may yet be better—saw within
A worthier image for the sanctuary,
And shaped it forth before the multitude

Divinely human, raising worship so
To higher reverence more mix'd with love—
That better self shall live till human Time
Shall fold its eyelids, and the human sky
Be gather'd like a scroll within the tomb
Unread for ever.
This is life to come,
Which martyr'd men have made more glorious
For us who strive to follow. May I reach
That purest heaven, be to other souls
The cup of strength in some great agony,
Enkindle generous ardour, feed pure love,
Beget the smiles that have no cruelty—
Be the sweet presence of a good diffused,
And in diffusion ever more intense.
So shall I join the choir invisible
Whose music is the gladness of the world.

Anne Brontë: 1820–1849

The least-read of the sisters, perhaps because she died so early of consumption. She was buried in Scarborough churchyard.

67 Lines composed in a Wood on a Windy Day

My soul is awakened, my spirit is soaring
  And carried aloft on the wings of the breeze;
For above and around me the wild wind is roaring,
  Arousing to rapture the earth and the seas.

The long withered grass in the sunshine is glancing,
  The bare trees are tossing their branches on high;
The dead leaves beneath them are merrily dancing,
  The white clouds are scudding across the blue sky.

I wish I could see how the ocean is lashing
  The foam of its billows to whirlwinds of spray;
I wish I could see how its proud waves are dashing,
  And hear the wild roar of their thunder to-day!

Jean Inglelow: 1820–1897

The *Encyclopaedia Britannica* gives so graphic an impression of this writer that we cannot do better than borrow it. 'Miss Inglelow was a woman of frank and hospitable manners, with a look of the Lady Bountiful of a country parish. She had nothing of the professional authoress or the "literary lady" about her and, as with characteristic simplicity she was accustomed to say, was no great reader.' She achieved a wide success with her *Poems* in 1863. Her verse was 'collected', as seems to be customary, in the year after her death.

68 For Exmoor

For Exmoor—
For Exmoor, where the red deer run, my weary heart doth cry:
She that will a rover wed, far her feet shall hie.
Narrow, narrow, shows the street, dull the narrow sky.
—Buy my cherries, whiteheart cherries, good my masters, buy!

For Exmoor—
O he left me, left alone, aye to think and sigh—
'Lambs feed down yon sunny coombe, hind and yearling shy
Mid the shrouding vapours walk now like ghosts on high'.
—Buy my cherries, blackheart cherries, lads and lasses, buy!

For Exmoor—
Hear my dear, why did ye so? Evil day have I;
Mark no more the antler'd stag, hear the curlew cry,
Milking at my father's gate while he leans anigh.
—Buy my cherries, whiteheart, blackheart, golden girls, O buy!

Adelaide Anne Procter: 1825–1854

She was a daughter of 'Barry Cornwall' (B.W. Procter), the poet and a friend of many poets 'from Bowles to Browning'. *Legends and Lyrics*, a book suited to the prevailing sentimentality of 1858, achieved nine editions in seven years. She wrote several popular hymns, and towards the end of her short life was received into the Catholic Church.

69 The Warrior to his Dead Bride

If in the fight my arm was strong
And forced my foes to yield,
If conquering and unhurt I come
Back from the battle-field—
It is because thy prayers have been
My safeguard and my shield.

Thy heart, my love, still beats in Heaven
With the same love divine
That made thee stoop to such a soul,
So hard, so stern, as mine—
My eyes have learnt to weep, Beloved,
Since last they look'd on thine.

I hear thee murmur words of peace,
Thro' the dim midnight air;
And a calm falls from the angel stars
And soothes my great despair—
The heavens themselves look brighter, Love,
Since thy sweet soul is there.

Christina Georgina Rossetti : 1830–1894

The late Sir Edmund Gosse wrote, 'Here was a cloistered spirit, timid, nun-like, bowed down by suffering and humility; her character was so retiring as to be almost invisible. All that we really need to know about her, save that she was a great saint, was that she was a great poet.' Ford Madox Ford, who set her as a poet far above her brother, Dante Gabriel Rossetti, would have endorsed the last five words of Sir Edmund's encomium: but the words 'great poet' should be used with extreme care. The 'suffering' was due to Grave's Disease which assailed the poet when she was forty.

Her father was a perfervid 'liberal', a mediocre poet (writing in Italian) and 'a subtle and original, if eccentric, commentator on Dante'. As an austere and handsome girl, she posed many times for her brother (e.g., in 'The Girlhood of Mary, Virgin'), Holman Hunt, Madox Brown and Millais. The Rossetti family was fond of competing in the composition of 'bout-rimés'—writing verses to a given set of rhymes—and it is easy to detect that some of this poet's published verses were so constructed.

70 Two Thoughts of Death

I

Her heart that loved me once is rottenness
  Now and corruption; and her life is dead
  That was to have been one with mine, she said.
The earth must lie with such a cruel stress
On eyes whereon the white lids used to press;
  Foul worms fill up her mouth so sweet and red;
  Foul worms are underneath her graceful head;
Yet these, being born of her from nothingness,
These worms are certainly flesh of her flesh.—
  How is it that the grass is rank and green
  And the dew-dropping rose is brave and fresh
Above what was so sweeter far than they?
Even as her beauty hath passed quite away,
  Theirs too shall be as though it had not been.

71 II

So I said underneath the dusky trees:
  But, because still I loved her memory,
  I stooped to pluck a pale anemone,
And lo my hand lighted upon heartease
Not fully blown: while with new life from these
  Fluttered a starry moth that rapidly
  Rose toward the sun: sunlighted flashed on me
Its wings that seemed to throb like heart-pulses.
Far far away it flew, far out of sight,—
  From earth and flowers of earth it passed away
As though it flew straight up into the light.
  Then my heart answered me: Thou fool, to say
  That she is dead whose night is turned to day,
And no more shall her day turn back to night.

72 From Metastasio

First, last, and dearest,
  My love, my own,
Thee best beloved,
  Thee love alone,
Once and for ever
  So love I thee.

First as a suppliant
  Love makes his moan,
Then as a monarch
  Sets up his throne:
Once and for ever—
  So love I thee.

73 Remember

Remember me when I am gone away,
  Gone far away into the silent land;
  When you can no more hold me by the hand,
Nor I half turn to go, yet turning stay.
Remember me when no more day by day
  You tell me of our future that you plann'd:
  Only remember me; you understand
It will be late to counsel then or pray.
Yet if you should forget me for a while
  And afterwards remember, do not grieve:
  For if the darkness and corruption leave
  A vestige of the thoughts that once I had,
Better by far you should forget and smile
  Than that you should remember and be sad.

74 Song

When I am dead, my dearest,
  Sing no sad songs for me;
Plant thou no roses at my head,
  Nor shady cypress tree:

Be the green grass above me
  With showers and dewdrops wet;
And if thou wilt, remember,
  And if thou wilt, forget.

I shall not see the shadows,
  I shall not hear the rain;
I shall not hear the nightingale
  Sing on, as if in pain;
And dreaming through the twilight
  That doth not rise nor set,
Haply I may remember,
  And haply may forget.

75 Love that is Dead and Buried

Love that is dead and buried, yesterday
  Out of his grave rose up before my face;
  No recognition in his look, no trace
Of memory in his eyes dust-dimmed and grey.
While I, remembering, found no word to say,
  But felt my quickened heart leap in its place;
  Caught afterglow thrown back from long sad days,
Caught echoes of all music passed away.
Was this indeed to meet? I mind me yet,
  In youth we met when hope and love were quick,
  We parted with hope dead, but love alive:
I mind me how we parted when heart-sick,
  Remembering, loving, hopeless, weak to strive:
Was this to meet? Not so, we have not met.

PART FOUR

Part Four

AT LEAST TEN of the nineteen writers in Part Four were Irish. At the turn of the century there was, if we except the vogue of Rudyard Kipling, no literary event comparable with the emergence of 'The Celtic Movement'—strongly propelled by the genius of W. B. Yeats. In the first years of the present century it was shameful to know nothing of Cuchulainn, Maeve, Deirdre and the Sidhe (Little People, or Fairies). Some of us even struggled to learn the formidable Irish language; and everyone was delighted a little later by George Moore's feline account of the Movement. Many young writers industriously searched the family pedigree for at least one or two Celtic ancestors and were only consoled when a cult of Dostoievski and Tchekov displaced the Celts.

The poets were not yet pining to be 'strong' at all costs. Indeed there is a still a lingering sentimentality in this Section together with that mild mysticism which was termed 'The Celtic Twilight'. In the work of 'A.E.' and his disciple, Eva Gore-Booth, the mysticism was profound and real. Even at its most tenuous it was at least a pleasant alternative to the objectivity of Kipling and the materialistic outlook of H. G. Wells and Arnold Bennett.

Mathilde Blind: 1841–1896

An enthusiastic advocate of the higher education of women. Her father was a Mannheim banker named Cohen, and she adopted the name Blind in admiration of her step-father, Karl Blind, an energetic supporter of the Liberal Movement in the Europe of his time. Her first book, *Poems by Claude Lake*, appeared in 1867. In 1890 she published a translation of Marie Bashkirtseff's remarkable *Journal*.

76 The Dead

The dead abide with us. Though stark and cold
    Earth seems to grip them, they are with us still:
  They have forged our chains of being for good or ill,
And their invisible hands these hands yet hold.
Our perishable bodies are the mould

In which their strong imperishable will—
Mortality's deep yearning to fulfil—
Hath grown incorporate through dim time untold.
Vibrations infinite of life in death,
As a star's travelling light survives its star!
So may we hold our lives that, when we are
The fate of those who then will draw this breath,
They shall not drag us to their judgment bar
And curse the heritage that we bequeath.

'Violet Fane' (Lady Currie, née Mary Montgomerie Lamb): 1843–1905

The two lyrics with which we represent this once well-known writer come from an unusual frame of mind—the fear, in the first, that the consummation of a high hope may bring separation, and the mingling, in the second, of a sad theme with a gay and pretty rhyme-pattern.

Her mother (Mary Montgomerie) was daughter and heiress of the eleventh Earl of Eglinton. The poet was twice married, first to a gentleman named Singleton.

77 A Foreboding

I do not dread an alter'd heart,
Or that long line of land or sea
Should separate my love from me,
I dread that drifting slow apart—
All unresisted, unrestrain'd—
Which comes to some when they have gain'd
The dear endeavour of their soul.

As two light skiffs that sail'd together,
Through days and nights of tranquil weather,
Adown some inland stream, might be
Drifted asunder, each from each;
When, floating with the tide, they reach
The hoped-for end, the promised goal,
The sudden glory of the sea.

78 A May Song

A little while my love and I,
Before the mowing of the hay,
Twined daisy-chains and cowslip-balls,
And caroll'd glees and madrigals,
Before the hay, beneath the may,
My love (who loved me then) and I.

For long years now my love and I
Tread sever'd paths to varied ends;
We sometimes meet, and sometimes say
The trivial things of every day,
And meet as comrades, meet as friends,
My love (who loved me once) and I.

But never more my love and I
Will wander forth, as once, together,
Or sing the songs we used to sing
In spring-time, in the cloudless weather:
Some cord is mute that used to ring,
Some word forgot we used to say
Amongst the may, before the hay,
My love (who loves me not) and I.

The Hon. Emily Lawless: 1845–1913

Daughter of Lord Cloncurry, she wrote several novels—and a book about the Aran Islands as they were in the 'eighties. Lady Gregory says 'she was very tall, with red-gold hair, full of laughter and humour. . . . An artist, a great walker, a horse-woman and a swimmer.' Her mother was so beautiful that 'once when she went into the House of Lords the assembly stood up in tribute to that beauty.'

79 Dirge of the Munster Forest, 1581

Bring out the hemlock! bring the funeral yew!
The faithful ivy that doth all enfold;
Heap high the rocks, the patient brown earth strew,
And cover them against the numbing cold.

Marshall my retinue of bird and beast,
Wren, titmouse, robin, birds of every hue;
Let none keep back, no, not the very least,
Nor fox, nor deer, nor tiny nibbling crew,
Only bid one of all my forest clan
Keep far from us on this our funeral day.
On the grey wolf I lay my sovereign ban,
The great grey wolf who scrapes the earth away,
Lest, with hook'd claw and furious hunger, he
Lay bare my dead for gloating foes to see—
Lay bare my dead, who died, and died for me.

For I must shortly die as they have died,
And lo! my doom stands yoked and link'd with theirs;
The axe is sharpen'd to cut down my pride:
I pass, I die, and leave no natural heirs,
Soon shall my sylvan coronals be cast;
My hidden sanctuaries, my secret ways,
Naked must stand to the rebellious blast;
No Spring shall quicken what this Autumn slays.
Therefore, while still I keep my russet crown,
I summon all my lieges to the feast.
Hither, ye flutters! black, or pied, or brown;
Hither, ye furr'd ones! Hither every beast!
Only to one of all my forest clan
I cry, 'Avaunt! Our mourning revels flee!'
On the grey wolf I lay my sovereign ban,
The great grey wolf with scraping claws, lest he
Lay bare my dead for gloating foes to see—
Lay bare my dead, who died, and died for me.

Lady Augusta Gregory (Persse): 1852–1932

Born in County Galway, Lady Gregory, who in 1903 seemed a massive and impressive person, will always be remembered for her long and noble friendship with W. B. Yeats. She wrote many plays that were liked for their Irish humour, and she was the dominant influence in the Abbey Theatre during its most brilliant period.

The two poems which follow are, of course, translations from the Irish. Mary Hynes was a famous village-beauty of more than a hundred years ago, and Raftery, who celebrates her, was a blind wandering ballad-maker.

80 Mary Hynes

There is a sweet air on the side of the hill
When you are looking down upon Baile-laoi;
When you are walking in the valley picking nuts and
  blackberries
There is music of the birds in it and music of the sidhe.

What is the worth of greatness till you have the light
Of the flower of the branch that is by your side?
There is no good to deny it or to try to hide it,
She is the sun in the heavens who wounded my heart.

There is no part of Ireland I did not travel
From the rivers to the tops of the mountains,
To the edge of Loch Greine whose mouth is hidden,
And I saw no beauty but was behind hers.

Her hair was shining and her brows were shining too;
Her face was like herself, her mouth pleasant and sweet.
She is my pride, and I give her the branch,
She is the shining flower of Baile-laoi.

(From the Irish of Raftery)

81 Donall Oge

It is late last night the dog was speaking of you,
The snipe was speaking of you in her deep marsh,
It is you are the lonely bird throughout the woods,
And that you may be without a mate until you find me.

You promised me and you said a lie to me,
That you would be before me where the sheep are flocked.
I gave a whistle and three hundred cries to you,
And I found nothing there by a bleating lamb.

You promised me a thing that was hard for you,
A ship of gold under a silver mast,
Twelve towns and a market in all of them,
And a fine white court by the side of the sea.

You promised me a thing that is not possible,
That you would give me gloves of the skin of a fish,
That you would give me shoes of the skin of a bird,
And a suit of the dearest silk in Ireland.

My mother said to me not to be talking with you,
To-day or to-morrow or on the Sunday.
It was a bad time she took for telling me that,
It was shutting the door after the house was robbed.

You have taken the east from me, you have taken the west
from me,
You have taken what is before me and what is behind me;
You have taken the moon, you have taken the sun from me,
And my fear is great you have taken God from me.

(From the Irish)

Margaret Woods: 1856–?

82 To the Forgotten Dead

To the forgotten dead,
Come, let us drink in silence ere we part.
To every fervent yet resolvèd heart
That brought its tameless passion and its tears,
Renunciation and laborious years,
To lay the deep foundations of our race,
To rear its mighty ramparts overhead
And light its pinnacles with golden grace.
To the unhonoured dead.

To the forgotten dead,
Whose dauntless hands were stretched to grasp the rein
Of Fate and hurl into the void again
Her thunder-hoofèd horses, rushing blind
Earthward along the courses of the wind.
Among the stars along the wind in vain
Their souls were scattered and their blood was shed,
And nothing, nothing of them doth remain.
To the thrice-perished dead.

83 Weep no more

Weep no more, for why should sorrow
Spend a time too short for kisses?
Wilt thou weep because to-morrow
Brings no hours so sweet as this is?
O fond heart!
Soon 'tis fled and then we part.

Comes no hour so sweet as this is—
Haste to harvest then such flow'rs
All thine hours
Keep the fragrance of its kisses.

Time but treads the slow sun's measure,
Lightning souls outstrip his fleetness,
Packing half a life-time's pleasure
In a moment of completeness.
Haste, O haste,
Ere such moments run to waste!

Soon shall come an hour for weeping,
Days enough and long to spare
For thy care,
And thy tears shall haunt thee sleeping.

Tears are longer than sweet laughter,
Yet they pass, and being ended,
Like a radiance following after
Stormy eyes from suns descended,
So their rain
Fades into this light again.

Dollie Radford: 1858–1917

She was dark, very small and of a most retiring disposition. Her husband, Ernest Radford, was a man of letters who attained some prominence toward the end of the nineteenth century, but in verse-craft his wife, though her gift was modest, excelled him.

84 Spring Song

Ah love, the sweet spring blossoms cling
To many a broken wind-tossed bough,
And young birds among branches sing
That mutely hung till now.

The little new-born things which lie
In dewy meadows, sleep and dream
Beside the brook that twinkles by
To some great lonely stream.

And children, now the day is cold,
From many a warm and cosy nest,
Look up to see the young moon hold
The old moon to her breast.

Dear love, my pulses throb and start
Tonight with longings sweet and new,
And young hopes beat within a heart
Grown old in loving you.

'*Michael Field*' (*no dates*)

This was the pseudonym of Miss Katherine Bradley and Miss Edith Cooper. Sturge Moore, introducing a 'Selection' of their poems, wrote: 'They had a wonderful reception in the eighties, announced by Browning and hailed as a major star, but their work, hurried by its welcome, disappointed this expectation, which was also dashed to discover that they were an aunt and a niece and not some man unknown, some Avatar of Waring. . . .'

Harold Monro, of The Poetry Bookshop, never slackened in his praise of their verse and plays.

85 Renewal

As the young phoenix, duteous to his sire,
Lifts in his beak the creature he has been,
And, lifting o'er the corse broad vans for screen,
Bears it to solitudes, erects a pyre,
And, soon as it is wasted by the fire,
Grids with disdainful claw the ashes clean;
Then spreading unencumber'd wings serene
Mounts to the aether with renew'd desire:

So joyously I lift myself above
The life I buried in hot flames today.
The flames themselves are dead: and I can range
Alone through the untarnish'd sky I love,
And trust myself, as from the grave I may,
To the enchanting miracles of change.

Amy Levy: 1861–1889

She was educated in Brighton and then spent four terms at Newnham College, Cambridge. Very soon after correcting the proofs of *A London Plane-Tree*, she committed suicide by suffocating herself with charcoal fumes. The coroner gave a verdict of 'self-destruction, cause unknown', but Dr. Richard Garnett believed that, being of a melancholy nature, she brooded over her increasing deafness and over family bereavements. She also seems to have dreaded that she might become insane. When we learn that Oscar Wilde referred to her as 'a girl of genius', we think at once of Dryden's couplet:

'How near to genius madness is allied;
A thin partition doth their bounds divide.'

86 A London Plane-Tree

Green is the plane-tree in the square,
The other trees are brown;
They droop and pine for country air;
The plane-tree loves the town.

Here from my garret-pane I mark
The plane-tree bud and blow,
Shed her recuperative bark,
And spread her shade below.

Among her branches, in and out,
The city breezes play;
The dull fog wraps her round about;
Above, the smoke curls grey.

Others the country take for choice,
And hold the town in scorn;
But she has listen'd to the voice
On city breezes borne.

87 London Poets

They trod the streets and squares where now I tread,
With weary hearts, a little while ago;
When, thin and grey, the melancholy snow
Clung to the leafless branches overhead;
Or when the smoke-veil'd sky grew stormy-red
In Autumn; with a re-arisen woe
Wrestled, what time the passionate spring-winds blow;
And paced scorch'd stones in summer. They are dead.

The sorrow of their souls to them did seem
As real as mine to me, as permanent.
To-day—it is the shadow of a dream,
The half-forgotten breath of breezes spent.
So shall another soothe his woe supreme—
No more he comes, who this way came and went.

Katharine Tynan: 1861–1919

A fecund novelist who seems to have published at least one novel every year between 1887 and 1919. She was educated at Sienna Convent, Drogheda: and she married a Mr. Hinkson in 1893.

88 Drought

The sky is grayer than doves,
Hardly a zephyr moves,
Little voices complain;
The leaves rustle before the rain.

No thrush is singing now,
All is still in the heart o' the bough;
Only the trembling cry
Of young leaves murmuring thirstily.

Only the moan and stir
Of little hands in the boughs I hear,
Beckoning the rain to come
Out of the evening, out of the gloom.

The wind's wings are still;
Nothing stirs but the singing rill
And hearts that complain.
The leaves rustle before the rain.

Mary Elizabeth Coleridge: 1862–1907

Her great grandfather was the elder brother of the great Samuel Taylor Coleridge. She had the high distinction of being praised by Robert Louis Stevenson and by the poet-laureate Robert Bridges. The latter said that 'her early verses are both beautiful and original, and often exhibit imagination of a very rare kind.' The decidedly 'original' poem which we have chosen will leave the student wondering in what way the subject of the poem had fallen from his pedestal. Perhaps he had too freely celebrated some occasion: perhaps he would have applauded Stevenson's lines:

'O graceful housemaid, tall and fair,
I love your shy imperial air,
And always loiter on the stair
When you are going by' . . .

We know that she was 'much influenced by Tolstoy, and exercised her gifts as a teacher with working-women at her home.'

89 Mortal Combat

It is because you were my friend,
I fought you as the devil fights.
Whatever fortune God may send,
For once I set the world to rights.

And that was when I thrust you down,
And stabbed you twice and twice again,
Because you dared take off your crown,
And be a man like other men.

Ethna Carbery (Anna Johnston): (?) 1875–1902

With her sister Alice Milligan (q.v.) she founded the patriotic Irish magazine *The Shan Van Vocht*. In 1900 she married the Donegal poet and novelist Seumas MacManus. Early in this century her verse brought a waft of desirable wildness into the sophisticated London poetry of that time.

90 The Sad Song of Finian

I was sent adrift on the waves of the world,
Ochón! ochón!
All for the sake of the yellow-curled
Slender girl that I wished my own.

I wandered East and I wandered West,
Ochón! ochón!
And never saw sloe-blossom white as her breast,
Though the heart in under is hard as stone.

I was scourged by the cruel Red Wind o' the Hills,
Ochón! ochón!
I lay all night in the mist that chills,
And to God and Mary I made my moan.

I saw through the dark her eyes aglow,
Ochón! ochón!
Shadowy, shimmering like the flow
Of running water o'er rock moss-grown.

I saw through the dark the shine of her hair,
Ochón! ochón!
It floated over and round me there—
A golden web down the silence blown.

I saw through the dark her rowan-hued lips,
Ochón! ochón!
Her cheek, soft-curving, whose young blush slips
Into the snow 'bove her kerchief shown.

My Star of Knowledge! my Flower of Grace!
Ochón! ochón!
'Tis she has left me in woeful case,
With empty arms to lament alone.

I wander North and I wander South,
Ochón! ochón!
In the veins of my heart is a burning drouth,
And love for her tortures my every bone.

I am adrift on the waves of the world—
Ochón! ochón!
Tossed by the storm, by the green seas whirled.
All for the sake of the yellow-curled
Slender girl that I wished my own.

Eva Selina Gore-Booth: 1870–1926

Yeats records having seen 'two beautiful figures among the great trees of Lissadell', the one being Eva Gore-Booth and the other her sister, the Countess Markievicz—a revolutionary whom some would call a fanatic. The poet is clearly a disciple, even an imitator, of 'A.E.'

91 Ecstasy

"God holds the soul attracted to him by its roots."
PLATO.

He who seeks God has yet no need of wings,
Down in the deeps of being a dim road
Leads through the soul unto the roots of things,
And that abyss that is the god's abode.

There in the enchanted caves of night,
And dim recesses of unconscious mind,
The Wise Men's Star burns with a steady light,
And a faint whisper lingers on the wind.

92 Unity

The primrose has her gentle root
A hundred miles beyond the sod,
Deep buried in the Absolute,
Safe in the inmost will of God.

The One Thing that is everything,
Is very close to grass and trees;
Hers is the song the satyrs sing,
The wild fern clings about her knees.

And Psyche's lamp, and Buddha's dream,
Those words that shall not fade or pass,
Are but the lilt of a lost stream
That flows under the world's grass.

Nora Hopper: 1871–1906

She was the daughter of a Captain in the 31st Bengal Native Infantry. In 1901 she married the literary critic, W. H. Chesson. According to *Who was Who* her Celtic sympathies were 'never strengthened by residence in Ireland.'

93 The Wind among the Reeds

Mavrone, Mavrone! the wind among the reeds,
It calls and cries, and will not let me be;
And all its cry is of forgotten deeds
When men were loved of all the Daoine-sidhe.

O Sidhe that have forgotten how to love,
And Sidhe that have forgotten how to hate,
Asleep 'neath quicken boughs that no winds move,
Come back to us ere yet it be too late.

Pipe to us once again, lest we forget
What piping means, till all the Silver Spears
Be wild with gusty music, such as met
Carolan once, amid the dusty years.

Dance in your rings again: the yellow weeds
You used to ride so far, mount as of old—
Play hide and seek with winds among the reeds,
And pay your scores again with fairy gold.

Dora Sigerson Shorter: 1870–1918

Dr. Sigerson, her father, was a well-known man of letters in Dublin. In 1896 she married the prolific journalist, Clement Shorter.

94 The Comforters

When I crept over the hill, broken with tears.
   When I crouched down on the grass, dumb in despair.
I heard the soft croon of the wind bend to my ears,
   I felt the light kiss of the wind touching my hair.

When I stood lone on the height my sorrow did speak,
   As I went down the hill, I cried and I cried,
The soft little hands of the rain stroking my cheek,
   The kind little feet of the rain ran by my side.

When I went to thy grave, broken with tears,
 When I crouched down in the grass, dumb in despair,
I heard the sweet croon of the wind soft in my ears,
 I felt the kind lips of the wind touching my hair.

When I stood by thy cross, sorrow did speak.
 When I went down the long hill, I cried and I cried.
The soft little hands of the rain stroked my pale cheek,
 The kind little feet of the rain ran by my side.

'Laurence Hope' : (no dates)

This writer, whose life was romantic in the extreme, has suffered seriously from the extravagant and sometimes derisive popularity of 'Less than the Dust' and 'Pale hands, pink-tipped. . . .' She was a better poet than an anti-romantic era will concede.

95 Kashmiri Song by Juma

You never loved me, and yet to save me,
One unforgettable night you gave me
Such chill embraces as the snow-covered heights
Receive from clouds, in northern, Auroral nights.
Such keen communion as the frozen mere
Has with immaculate moonlight, cold and clear.
And all desire,
Like failing fire,
Died slowly, faded surely, and sank to rest
Against the delicate chillness of your breast.

Mary W. Findlater: b. 1865

Mrs. Findlater, who affirms that she will soon or never be eighty-two, denies that she should be regarded as a 'living' poet; but although 'Annie Ferguson' has accumulated the respectable 'crust' of more than fifty years, Mary Findlater's lines about the caterpillars and the butterflies date from 1943.

She is one of the poets who vehemently resented the original title of our book, but also one who, fortunately, shrugged her shoulders. 'Only Mrs. Hemans could have thought of it,' says she, 'and what roistering rhymes would you expect if you bought a book called *Masculine Poetry*?'

The time may have come when 'feminine' will not suggest feebleness or 'masculine' suggest 'a song of bawdry'.

96 Annie Ferguson

She died last night: (*How deep the Snows of May*
Bloom on the thickets there.) See how her face
Is blindly turned against the light. (*The grass*
Of Spring comes new—as it was yesterday
And ever shall be.) They have put away
Her hands beneath the sheet. (*How green the place,*
See thro' the leaves white butterflies that chase
Each other in the sun.) O poor dead clay!

The mouth is silent and the eyes are blind!
(*But how the young leaves in the sun and shade*
Do tremble with the faint delicious wind!)
Her life is ended and her grave is made.
And is this all that Death can leave behind!
Good Lord deliver me! I am afraid!

97 The Ape and the Key

'For so foolish was I, and ignorant: I was as a Beast before Thee.'—Psalm lxxiii. 22.

'Now a little before it was day . . . Christian as one half amazed, broke out into this passionate speech:

'"What a fool", quoth he, "am I, to lie in a stinking dungeon when I may as well walk at liberty! *I have a key in my bosom called Promise, that will, I am persuaded, open any lock in Doubting Castle.*" '—*Pilgrims Progress.*

I

They locked his cage; and through the bars
They gave an Ape the key:
From noon until he saw the stars,
Hour after hour sat he,
Still fumbling with the key.

He shook it, smelt it, pried about,
All baffled and confused;
He never found the secret out
Of how the key was used,
Tho' long he sat and mused.

And men, his captors, paused to mock
(As still he pried and scanned),
The Beast that fuddled with the lock,
But could not understand
Freedom was in his hand!

Yet there—to him, half-Beast, half-Man,
Some far remembrance came,
Of life before his days began
In that stale cage of shame:
Of savage joys that once he knew
When he ran with his kind:
Of raids on fields of fruits and dew:
Of refuge he might find
In forests deep and blind.

* * *

II

I, too, imprisoned: walled apart:
When I kneel down to pray,
Hold always in my darkened heart
A secret hope that may
Turn darkness into day.

'Twould fit the door at which I knock
If I could prove it true,
Like a key of gold in a silver lock,
And let my soul pass through.
Yet—tho' the Oracles be dumb,
And tho' I cannot see—
To me, as to the Ape, there come
Hints of what light might be,
If once the soul got free.

For I have felt the wind that stirred
The woods when Spring's begun;
And I have seen the rose: and heard
The mountain waters run:
And watched the rising sun.

Yes—and a deeper sign than those
(Tho' hidden from the wise)—
The faith of Infancy—that knows
The love that stills its cries;
The breast whereon it lies.

So I believe . . . and then I doubt:
I wonder day by day:
I never find the secret out
'God will not—or he may?'
Bewildered, *still I pray*.

98 Caterpillars' Conversation

'Are you afraid of change—of Death?'
One grub to another saith.
'Because I am: that little room
Our Brother made was just a tomb!
I watched, and when I saw him creep
Therein, and wind himself to sleep
I knew he was completely gone
From this Vast Leaf we feed upon.'

The second answered 'Not so I!
He did not weave his shroud to die,
For one day as I crawled inside
That room, I saw its walls divide
And out came he—there was a change
Into someone fair and strange.
He spread bright wings and then he flew
Up, up, into the warmth and blue,
No more a grub like me and you!
Away from this dark Leaf of ours
Where the whole tribe crawls and devours.'

'What's wrong with grubs?' the first one said,
'You've got some notion in your head.
We're all alike, and our poor Brother
Was just a grub, like any other,
And now we know that he is gone
From this Vast Leaf we feed upon.'

The second answered 'Ah, but I
Once heard a story from a Fly,
Who told me that when he had been
Far up, above us, he had seen
A land all honey and scents and flowers,
A better country than this of ours
Where the whole tribe crawls and devours.'

His listener laughed—'The same old lies!
Told since the flood by Birds and Flies.
I've heard a very different tale
Once from a most experienced Snail—
One who knew all there was to know
And who had travelled far, tho' slow—
'Twas he who told me Birds and Flies
Were always boasting, telling lies,
The idle senseless, buzzing things!'
'*What need or use have we for wings?*

We crawl so well' he said ('I've heard
He since was eaten by a bird!')
But he had journeyed far to find
What truth—if any—lay behind
Their boastings—meeting day by day
With myriad dangers on the way
He crawled, until he reached the edge
Of our Vast Leaf, where, from a ledge
He looked below, above, around
And utter emptiness he found—
Nothing but nothingness, though he
With eyes on stalks, of course, could see
Much farther into space than we,
'At last,' he said, 'The truth was out',
Proved by himself beyond a doubt—
'Nothing exists but what we know'
Where then, could our poor Brother go
Because we see that he is gone
From this Vast Leaf we feed upon'?

The second asked 'But could your Friend
Even with his eyes on stalks—pretend
To see Beginning from the End?
The night is black and blind, yet mark!
The dayspring rises after dark.
Our Brother did not pause to tell
The way he went—he knew it well—
And as he rose beyond my sight
Seemed going forward into light.
Whither he went I do not know
Only that he rejoiced to go.
I watched him till my eyes grew dim
And fain would I have followed him!
Away from this dark Leaf of ours
Where the whole tribe crawls and devours.'

Moira O'Neill

The following lyric (in which 'the sun goes down at seven') was greatly liked in England, as well as Ireland, in the first decade of this century. It has been set to music by several composers.

99 The Fairy Lough

Loughareema, Loughareema
  Lies so high among the heather;
A little lough, a dark lough,
  The wather's black an' deep.
Ould herons go a-fishing there,
  An' seagulls all together
Float roun' the one green island
  On the fairy lough asleep.

Loughareema! Loughareema!
  When the sun goes down at seven,
When the hills are dark an' *airy*,
  'Tis a curlew whistles sweet!
Then somethin' rustles all the reeds
  That stand so thick and even;
A little wave runs up the shore
  An' flees as if on feet.

Loughareema! Loughareema!
  Stars come out, an' stars are hidin';
The wather whispers on the stones,
  The flittherin' moths are free.
One'st before the mornin' light
  The Horseman will come ridin'
Roun' and roun' the fairy lough,
  An' no one there to see!

ALICE MILLIGAN

Alice Milligan

She contributed individual work to 'The Celtic Movement'. Now—in a remote part of Ireland—she seems to be inaccessible even by post.

100 When I was a little Girl

When I was a little girl,
In a garden playing,
A thing was often said
To chide us delaying:

When after sunny hours,
At twilight's falling,
Down through the garden walks
Came our old nurse calling.

'Come in! for it's growing late,
And the grass will wet ye!
Come in! or when it's dark
The Fenians will get ye.'

Then, at this dreadful news,
All helter-skelter,
The panic-struck little flock
Ran home for shelter.

And round the nursery fire
Sat still to listen,
Fifty bare toes on the hearth,
Ten eyes a-glisten.

To hear of a night in March,
And loyal folk waiting,
To see a great army of men
Come devastating.

An army of Papists grim,
With a green flag o'er them,
Red-coats and black police
Flying before them.

But God (Who our nurse declared
Guards British dominions)
Sent down a deep fall of snow
And scattered the Fenians.

'But somewhere they're lurking yet,
Maybe they're near us,'
Four little hearts pit-a-pat
Thought 'Can they hear us?'

Then the wind-shaken pane
Sounded like drumming;
'Oh!' they cried, 'tuck us in,
The Fenians are coming!'

Four little pairs of hands
In the cots where she led those
Over their frightened heads
Pulled up the bedclothes.

But one little rebel there,
Watching all with laughter,
Thought 'When the Fenians come
I'll rise and go after.'

Wished she had been a boy
And a good deal older—
Able to walk for miles
With a gun on her shoulder.

Able to lift aloft
The Green Flag o'er them
(Red-coats and black police
Flying before them).

And, as she dropped asleep,
Was wondering whether
God, if they prayed to Him,
Would give fine weather.

Susan L. Mitchell

Was for a good many years Secretary to the poet-painter-visionary, George Russell (A.E.). Nevertheless the reader will note that he influenced Eva Gore-Booth, as a writer, more than he influenced his secretary. Susan Mitchell wrote admirable verses of gentle satire about the great figures of the Irish literary renaissance.

101 The Descent of the Child

Who can bring back the magic of that story,
  The singing seraphim, the kneeling kings,
The starry path by which the Child of Glory
  'Mid breathless watchers and through myriad wings
Came, with the heaven behind Him slowly waning,
  Dark with His loss, unto the brightening earth,
The young ennobled star, that He, so deigning,
  Chose for the heavenly city of His birth?
What but the heart of youth can hold the story,
  The young child's heart, so gentle and so wild,
It can recall the magic of that Glory
  That dreamed Itself into a little child.

PART FIVE

PART V

Part Five

MANY YEARS HAVE gone by since Jane Austen, if anybody entered her room, modestly concealed the immortal pages on which she was at work. Right up to the first decade of this century it was considered ill-bred for a 'young lady' to receive money for her art. At that time, for example, a talented girl-painter who was in Cairo with her military father shewed two pictures at an exhibition, but her parents refused to let her accept any money when somebody bought the paintings. Women have always been allowed to publish verse, perhaps because it is not a highly saleable commodity and also because it was regarded, like 'sketching' and harp-playing, as an elegant accomplishment. Then, too, society began in the middle of the nineteenth century to let women receive money for novel-writing: but it is not easy now to recapture a sense of the life-limitations which were imposed upon women until our own time.

The reader will recognise at once how it is in this part of the book that the poets reveal in full their infinite variety. Sentimentality (not confined to their sex) has completely disappeared, and the poems though often tragic are never lachrymose. What do we find? A notable number of poems inspired by flowers, children, animals and the wreckage produced by war. We perceive also an oscillation between strict metrical forms and the fashionable looseness of line which is probably symptomatic of a restless and inharmonious era. In particular we find a marked use of the severe sonnet-form. Could this be due, I wondered, to the neatness which characterises most women? My collaborator replied that, on the contrary, 'it is because our minds are *not* tidy, and the poets like to be self-disciplined.' Certainly women were the best letter-writers because they were discursive and did not keep grimly to the mere 'point' of a letter. The reader will also note, I expect, that women-poets have frequently a twinkle in the eye as though they cannot always take life solemnly.

The writers are ranged in alphabetical order; and since it would be an impertinence for me to rank them, as if they were lawn-tennis players, I will make a flying reference to each as her work arrives on the page.

Jane Barton

We begin this Part with a poem in which there is no 'twinkle', but it obviously came from a deep and poignant experience, and it illustrates another characteristic of good modern verse—that, sad though it is, the poem suggests self-reliance and a will to overcome disillusion.

102 Grief must go

This I will pray—
To be contented with the less,
Remain unhurt by love's duress,
Not to feel heart and soul rebel
When to myself I bleakly tell,
'This then is all he has to say
Or give to me once loved so well'.

So will I pray—
For I am in the midst of days
That reach out to a flattened edge,
Drearily sliding down to death,
Empty of even a ghostly breath
Of the love we made together.

Lost aspirations of my youth
—So finely sprung and tended fair—
Mock me and poison every hour;
Yet in the misery I bear
Still I will pray—
To be contented with the less,
Be proof and strong for evermore
Against love's cold and cruel duress.

Vera Bax

A writer who also is a portrait-painter. She was a successful student at the South Kensington School of Art. Her facility in verse is exceptional, and she is one who writes more often in sonnet form than in any other. The stoical dignity of the two following sonnets is characteristic.

103 The Suicides

Their souls escaped from Earth and fled;
They were so glad that they were dead,
And, softly as two feathers blown,
They soared away from pain and tears
Into the strange and vast unknown;
Forgetting all the weary years
When life, that held no ray of hope,
Had galled them like a hempen rope.
They floated in a golden light,
Each seeing but the other's face;
All else was hidden from their sight,
While time stood still in boundless space.

Ah, was it aeons that had past,
Or moments, when a voice at last
From out the blessed silence spake?
'Return, rash souls, to Earth,' it cried,
'How dared you thus my chalice break,
'Or dream my will could be defied!
'Two children now to woe are born,
'Take you their shapes, and do not scorn
'To drain life's bitter cup, but pray
'That strength, not happiness, be giv'n,
'And light to guide you on the way;
'There is no easy path to heav'n.'

On Earth two babes, uneasy, slept:
Each started with a cry, and wept.

104 April, 1941

Beauty, your name sounds strange and sad,
Like that of an old lover;
Bewildered in a world gone mad,
Our ears can scarce discover
Your music fluting faint and far;

Gone the radiance of your face
That shone on Athens like a star,
And gave her children grace.
You drift forlornly, pale, remote,
With your own tears empearled,
Weeping for the Greece that wrote
Your name across the world.

105 To Richard

(Killed in action, 17th August, 1942)

I hide my grief throughout the weary days,
And gather up the threads of life again,
Remembering you ever gave your praise
To those for whom fate's hardest thrust was vain.
Now, when I feel my courage flicker low,
Your spirit comes to breathe it into flame,
Until I lift my head, and smiling go,
Whispering softly your belovéd name.
And yet to me it seems but yesterday
You were a child, and full of childish fears;
Then I would run to you and soothe away
The loneliness of night, and dry your tears;
But now you are the comforter, and keep,
From out the shadows, watch, lest I should weep.

106 Christmas, 1943

Now Christmas comes again, to find my heart
Still as the frozen landscape: cold and still.
Like an automatum I play my part,
To noisy merriment must bend my will;
Yet how can I be glad, remembering,
Though all my tears so long ago were shed?
I would, in solitude, let fancy wing
Back through the past to that poor manger-bed,
Where gladness shone in such a night as this,
And holy peace descended for a while;

No laughter, loud and mirthless, marred its bliss,
No grief was there to hide behind a smile;
Only an innocence, a hope, a gleam:
A star that beckoned, and a woman's dream.

Sybil Horatia Calverley

She is a great-niece of the celebrated and inimitable C. S. Calverley. In fact she is a daughter of the late John Selwin Calverley and the late Sybil Isabella Disraeli. 'Dizzy' was her other great-uncle.

Here we come upon the first of our poems about 'non-humans', a gay lyric of congratulation to the so-often-unlucky worm and of censure upon the 'silly sleepy snail'. Horatia Calverley has worked enthusiastically in the cause of intelligent Drama.

107 Midsummer

Burnt lawns and iron-bound pastures
Perplex the feeding thrushes;
All day in the shrubbery bushes
They beat on their anvil stone;
A firm staccato tapping,
A quick unhurried trapping
Of many a silly sleepy snail
Who thinks he lives in a coat of mail
And closes his door with a seal of slime—
'Too late, too late, it's feeding time'
Says the busy bird with a beak like a flail,
As he beats on his anvil stone.
All quiet and cool, the tranquil worm
Lies under the earth so hard and firm,
No probing bird disturbs that crust.
But overhead in the heat and dust,
To the four winds the shells are thrown
By the thrush who beats on his anvil stone.

Frances Cornford

A fine flower of Cambridge culture, she is probably best known by her cameo-poem which begins, 'A young Apollo, golden-haired'. A line in that epigram—'the long littleness of life'—has almost joined the national proverbs and sayings; but 'In the Backs', a poem which holds an elusive mood in a subtle web of words, not one of which is unnecessary, will give the shock of authentic poetry to innumerable readers who are not yet born.

In the present group of verses we see her hesitating between a suspicion that life is 'futile' and 'absurd', and a sense, rarely absent in a serious poet, that mundane life is not the only mode of human consciousness.

108 The New-Born Baby's Song

When I was twenty inches long,
I could not hear the thrushes' song;
The radiance of morning skies
Was most displeasing to my eyes.

For loving looks, caressing words,
I cared no more than sun or birds;
But I could bite my mother's breast,
And that made up for all the rest.

109 No Immortality

Can it be possible, when we grow old
And Time destroys us, that the image of you,
Who brought to all, serenely, like a gift,
The eternal beauty of youth—as though you had lain,
A moment since, in English grass by the river,
Thinking and dreaming under the fresh sky
When May was in the hedges—can it be
This unique image of you, yourself, your smile,
(Which kept a secret sweetness, like a child's,
Though you might be most sad), your frowning eyes,

Must, when we die, in the vast air of Time
Be swallowed? Nothing, not a ghost, remain
To the revolving, hard, enamelled world
(For ever full of fears and births and deaths
And busyness) of all you were?
Perhaps
A thousand years ago some Greek boy died,
So lovely-bodied, so adored, so young.
Like us they wept, and treasured little things,
And laughed with tears, remembering his laughter,
And there was friendship in the very sound
Of his forgotten name to them. But now,
Now we know nothing; nothing is richer now
Because of all he was.
O you we have loved,
Can it be so with you? and, if it can,
How futile, how absurd the life of man!

110 Pre-Existence

I laid me down upon the shore
And dreamed a little space;
I heard the great waves break and roar;
The sun was on my face.

My idle hands and fingers brown
Played with the pebbles grey;
The waves came up, the waves went down,
Most thundering and gay.

The pebbles, they were smooth and round
And warm upon my hands,
Like little people I had found
Sitting among the sands.

The grains of sand so shining-small
Soft through my fingers ran;
The sun shone down upon it all,
And so my dream began:

How all of this had been before;
   How ages far away
I lay on some forgotten shore
   As here I lie to-day.

The waves came shining up the sands,
   As here to-day they shine;
And in my pre-pelasgian hands
   The sand was warm and fine.

I have forgotten whence I came,
   Or what my home might be,—
Or by what strange and savage name
   I called that thundering sea.

I only know the sun shone down
   As it still shines to-day,
And in my fingers long and brown
   The little pebbles lay.

III In the Backs

Too many of the dead—some I knew well—
Have smelt this unforgotten river smell
Liquid and old and dank,
And on the tree-dark, lacquered slowly-passing stream
Have seen the boats come softly as in dream
Past the green bank.
So Camus, reverend Sire, came footing slow
Three hundred years ago;
And Milton paced the avenue of trees
In miracle of sun and shade as now,
The dear, magnificent, unborn cadences
Behind his youthful brow.

Milton and Chaucer, Herbert, Herrick, Gray,
Rupert, and you forgotten others, say:
Are there slow rivers and bridges where you have gone away?

What new absorption have your spirits found,
What wider lot?
Some days in Spring do you come back at will
And tread with weightless feet the ancient ground?
O say, if not,
Why is this air so sacred and so still?

Eleanor Farjeon

belongs to a much-talented family. Her father was B. L. Farjeon, a successful Dickensian novelist, and she is a sister of the well-known musician, of Joseph Jefferson Farjeon, story-teller and playwright, and of the late Herbert Farjeon, revue-writer and Dramatic Critic. Their mother was an American lady of Jeffersonian descent.

It is forty years since I first read the chime-of-bells about the 'Broken-hearted gentleman' and for me those frivolous wenches are still tripping it, though according to the text they may now have encountered the calamities which the gentleman, a little spitefully, prognosticated.

This joyous lyric is followed by two tragic poems, and both are profoundly feminine: or could Stephen Phillips have imagined 'Farewell, you children'? Let us recall the fine speech of Lucrezia in his 'Paolo and Francesca', beginning

'Spared! to be spared what I was born to have!
I am a woman, and this very flesh
Demands its natural pangs, its rightful throes,
And I implore with vehemence those pains. . . .'

As for 'The Outlet', it has the high distinction of being one of the very few poems which did not contribute to the 'emotional hitch' in the young gentleman who rejected my proposed broadcast.

112 The Dance Ring

It was the middle of the spring
I saw three girls dance in a ring.

One was golden as the day,
Around her neck bright tresses lay.

One as hazel-nuts was brown
And to her feet her hair fell down.

One was black as midnight sky,
Her locks were like a crown piled high.

'Sweetings, shall I with ye fling?
It is the middle of the spring.'

I heard the three together sing:
'No man shall break our dancing ring.'

'Sweetings, that ye cannot tell—
Unkind sweetings, fare ye well.'

Then each a mocking kiss did blow:
'Give us presents ere you go.'

'You that the morning-glow outvie
For all my gift shall take a sigh.

'To you that like the ebbing year
In russet, go I give a tear.

'With you that seem of night to weave
Your grace a broken heart I leave.'

Then as from them I turned my feet
I listened how they laughèd sweet:

And 'Fare you well,' their laughter ran,
'Broken-hearted gentleman.'

But shoulder-over I did call:
'Dance on, ye scornful sweetings all.

'When I am lost in shadows grey
My gifts ye shall not fling away.

'While still the spring beneath your feet
Flows green your ring shall stand complete.

'But when the year begins to turn
My gifts to use ye well shall learn.

'And one shall sigh and one shall weep
And one shall crave eternal sleep.'

It was the middle of the spring
I saw three girls dance in a ring.

One was a yellow rose new-blown,
One as hazel-nuts was brown,
One she wore a midnight crown.

(My heart is still a-hungering.)

113 Sonnet

Farewell, you children that I might have borne.
Now must I put you from me year by year,
And year by year the root of life be torn
Out of this womb to which you were so dear;

Now year by year the milky springs be dried
Within the sealed-up fountains of my breast,
Now year by year be to my arms denied
The burden they would break with and be blessed.
Sometimes I felt your lips and hands so close
I almost could have plucked you from the dark,
But now your very dream more distant grows
As my still aching body grows more stark.
I shall not see you laugh or hear you weep,
Kiss you awake, or cover up your sleep.

114 The Outlet

Grief struck me. I so shook in heart and wit,
I thought I must speak of it or die of it.

A certain friend I had with strength to lend:
When mine was spent I went to find my friend,

Who, rising up with eyes wild for relief,
Hung on my neck and spoke to me of grief.

I raked the ashes of my burned-out strength
And found one coal to warm her with at length.

I sat with her 'til I was icy cold;
At last I went away, my grief untold.

Virginia Graham

A daughter of the late Harry Graham, one of our wittiest verse-writers. She is a well-known contributor to *Punch*. According to herself she is 'married to Antony Thesiger, worked full time from 1939 to 1946 with the Women's Voluntary Services; has no children, is a confirmed Cockney, is happiest in the theatre, and is musical.'

115 The Bridge, St. James's Park

You cannot find comfort in ducks.
Stoop to look into those beady brown eyes,
and they will tell you nothing.
Lean over the bridge and the reflected leaf-brown skies
quiver and fade as the little copper head
swims to your shadow;
and as he looks jauntily at the pond's bed
over that soft grey breast of his, you think
this duck knows something.
I am standing at the brink
of some sweet secret which will bountifully bless.

From the quirk of his tail I shall learn gaiety,
and though I cannot caress
the velvet roundness of his feathered hair,
I shall see in it the perfection of small things,
beauty of burnished copper warming the air,
satin-smooth order in the midst of confusion.
But in those flat eyes there lies no understanding or hope,
only a deadly cynicism, an utter disillusion.
You cannot find comfort in ducks.

Kathleen Hewitt

The daughter of an eccentric, lovable clergyman who on one occasion prevented a panic by 'skepping a swarm of bees' at Liverpool Street Station. This we learn from her autobiography, *The Only Paradise* (memory), a book that demonstrates without self-consciousness how pluckily a woman can fend for herself in a society predominantly masculine. She is well known as a novelist, and perhaps the best of her many novels is *Pattern in Yellow*. It records experiences in one of the less sophisticated parts of Africa where vegetation can only be described by the word—'lush'—a word which always seems to upset stay-at-home reviewers. Her few poems suggest a romantic nature which has devised for itself a carapace of cynicism: but here is not 'a deadly cynicism, an utter disillusion' like that to which the foregoing poet referred.

116 Silhouette

Your silhouette against the dappled sky
Was etched in steel, thus was the memory
Upon the tablets of the undiscerned
And future years indelibly deep-burned
Beneath the patina to be imposed:

The fingers of the sun were wide unclosed,
Mesmeric over weary earth they cast
A spell on fearfulness, itself aghast—
A serpent drugged in that lush ambience
With fangs indrawn. The very transcience

Of that enchantment exercised its thrall
In dwindling hours on thoughts beyond recall
That ebbed to silence.
Foolish it may be
To conjure symbols from a fantasy:
Yet ominous upon serrated stone
I saw your broken shadow, darkly thrown . . .

Sara Jackson

The twinkle in the eye is clearly perceptible in 'Lily McQueen'—an admirable example of a piece for which an appropriate metre has been found. The rhythm dances. Beckmesser would have given Sara Jackson a bad mark for the false rhyme 'over' and 'Cordova', though she is not the only modern poet, as we shall see, who would have distressed him in this way, but even he might have been assuaged by the image of Lord Oliver caprioling over to the irresistible Lily. We do not often find a poet who in the next breath, as it were, can produce a poem so different as the mystical 'Spiritus Sanctus'.

117 Lily McQueen

(A ballet. Pas de Deux)

Cool as a cucumber,
Cucumber, cucumber,
In belled, swaying muslin
Waltzed Lily McQueen:

But the eye of Lord Oliver,
(Wicked Lord Oliver)
The eye of Lord Oliver
Burnt grass from the green.

As he caprioled over
And over and over,
As he caprioled over
The daisies between.

'Find a rhyme for this lady,
This water-clear maidy,
Find a rhyme this lorn lady
To shield from the sun!'

And the eyes of Miss Lily
Dipped daffadowndilly,
While her round lips grew stilly
And shaped to a 'Come!'

As she leapt from her lover
With swoon and recover
Lest he should discover
Her secret was one

That was known the world over,
From Cork to Cordova,
That love burns a candle
More fierce than the sun.

So they twined in a tangle
Of love-lyric spangle
As the music's bright jangle
Emblazoned their song

That was older and bolder
Than his look as he told her
That passion's bright smoulder
Beat his heart like a gong!

Oh! such flowery, bowery,
Sunshine and showery
Peace of love's dowry
Will never be seen,

As when Frederick Oliver
(Wicked Lord Oliver)
Caprioled over
To Lily McQueen.

118 Spiritus Sanctus

I am the leaf,
Beauty; the sun's silk light;
A beggar left to burn
Unrobbed by night.

I am the twig;
The sharpness of the thorn
Piercing with passionate crown
Christ's living dawn.

I am the water;
The sad rain of life
Weeping the world's woe,
Solace of strife.

I am the bone;
The bled, enduring bride
Of the white, perishing flesh;
Sole heir and pride.

I am the thought,
The purpose and the peace;
The arrowed hand of God,
Pointing release.

From first awakening
To last lying down
I, His Spirit am.
The dying drown

In my wave,
To mount the seventh time
Eternally, where bides
The riddle and the rhyme.

Wrenne Jarman

Has recently published her first book of poems. In nearly all her work there are choice and curious phrases. The end of 'Valedictory' and the latter part of the feministic and finely-sustained 'Letter to Claudia' help to give her an honoured place among Roman Catholic poets. The insanities of war have elicited some of her noblest verse—and in 'The Neutral' there is again that feminine twinkle. Here is a highly distinctive poet who will some day be triumphantly 'discovered' by an influential journalist.

119 Plastic Airman

His face is smooth as sculptured faces are,
His features fair enough to draw a girl's
Arch backward glance, his disciplined blond curls
Swept from a grafted brow without a scar.

But this young mottled face does not betray,
As other faces do, the moods behind—
If he has secrets, they are locked away:
He looks out at the world from a drawn blind
Screening the man he was. And who was he?
Only the grave eyes know, and do not tell. . . .

Be gentle with him, World, who has foregone
His unique pattern, his identity:
Be tender, lest the frozen mask should melt
Abruptly, and surprise us with its scorn.

120 Valedictory

(*To the memory of Laurence Binyon, Stephen Haggard, William Soutar, Sidney Keyes, Alun Lewis, Keith Douglas, Richard Spender, Stephen Vincent Benet and Caleb Young Rice, 1943.*)

Of all the fated company who passed
This year, nine poets died—nine natural kings
Who had transfixed the flash of rainbow wings,
And felt a wild heart beat, and held it fast.

They gathered the old wonder, breathed into
It modern virtue they alone could lend,
And went down into darkness, to the end
Singing the primal beauty that they knew.

What does it matter if some had grown old,
Dim-eyed and wistful in the quest for truth,
While others gave their hot blood and their youth
So that the epic splendid might be told?
Salute, astronomers who find, afar,
Gleaming and glowing, a new nine-pointed star!

121 Letter to Claudia

These sad last days, dear Claudia, which have brought
The death in action of your single son,
Press heavily on an affectionate heart
To breathe condolences, but I'll refrain,
Knowing no touch can reach you where you go
In the numb coil of your immediate woe.

We grew together, peering hopefully out
From the safe window of our grounded ark
High on the silver slopes of Ararat
The while the so-called final dove evoked
Wide curves about us with its olive leaf.
(At least it bore the semblance of a leaf.)

That world was all we hoped; no fiercer birds
Screamed of calamity—that is, for us,
Nor did we fear the first drab wandering clouds
Though others seemed to find them ominous.
The powers we wielded needed no franchise—
We had our sex, our shining hair, our eyes.

Only occasionally did ghosts not lie—
Do you remember, Claudia, long ago
How Livia said, I'll not have children, I—
I'll bear no brats for cannon-fodder, *No!*
And you—laughed softly, thereby tempting Fate
To lead you deviously to this black gate.

The years went slowly, dropping on your boy
A pearly cortex hardening the child,
Giving a manlier glint to his straight eye,
A whiter burnish to his knightly shield.
You were so proud—not knowing yet, in wait
Beyond your door, the old Herodian hate.

The pot began to simmer. War in the East. . . .
Then, nearer home, a curious war in Spain.
Communist, fascist: Fascist, communist—
What could they offer us but an old pain?
And still the unicorn abstained the pool.
And still the boys went in and out of school.

Then Munich—pawnshop of the decencies
Our fathers had redeemed: infamous shrine
Of vain appeasing silly sophistries—
And all that year the dreadful long decline
That knew of no physician and no cure,
To total night whose sunrise was not sure.

Through all the long ordeal you put up
A front of calm indifference on the brink,
Pretending as you drained the poisoned cup
You toyed with milk and did not care to drink.
With steady hands, when all the world was fire,
You pushed your callow Isaac to the pyre. . . .

You, Claudia, home-woman, have not seen
Beyond the factory's barred and guarded door
The women at death-grips with the machine
Whirring to win the war within the war:
Not seen the lines of girls, their soft breasts bruised
Against the bench's edge, strangely misused—

These slim hands riveting, you would agree,
Were better fixing curls or flowers or frills:

Those oil-splashed dimpled arms conceivably
Could slake a gentler thirst than a steel drill's,—
Their bright escaping hair, their cornflower eyes
Showing only patience and a faint surprise. . . .

This is the hand our time has dealt us—lies,
Privation, labour, bloody tears and death.
So-called Dark Ages?—floodlit centuries
Compared with this once-vaunted twentieth.
Such is our generation's deal, my friend;
The pack was labelled 'Progress'—to what end?

And now I come, though halting, to my point,
Which is, that through our female indolence,
Our easy confluence to the natural bent,
We have laid safety at the shrine of sense
Entrusting government to the dominant male,
Who, albeit charming, is incapable.

I will make Man in my own image. . . . Straight
And truly god-like, this brave being confounds
Our fair intelligence, and as his right
Assumes the mastery of the hunting-grounds.
And if we do presume to question this
Supremacy, he quietens with a kiss.

He to his pleasant person adds the lure
Of glittering history, and science,—less
For War, says he, than for disease's cure—
And vast philosophies that might impress
But that for modest ends suffices still
A little Sermon uttered from a hill.

This shimmering guileless moonshine might be passed
But that a more sinister beam is found
To gloss the waste of war,—no medal cast
Could staunch you bleeding from your mortal wound.
Of what use glory, since it cannot heal?
Men are but dreamers: only we are real.

This ever-recurring and eternal grief
Of mourning Rachel sad past comforting,
The bare branch stricken and the trodden leaf,
It is the common, not the exceptional thing—
And will be, till all women, seeing clear
With one panoptic Cyclops eye, shall tear,

As vengeful serpents tore Laocoon.
The rotted veils of Man's misgovernment
Into their shameful shreds, and raise upon
The heaps of filthy spray with one consent
A Western matriarchy. Let those whom
A womb governs, govern by the womb. . . .

If this is dreaming, it was dreamed long since
In Sparta. The millennia could spare
One fleeting age to compensate our pains.
Meanwhile, dear Claudia, try not to wear
Your grief too sombrely for that lost dear
Child you will find again, although not here.

122 The Neutral

As I was walking in the Park
I met a blackbird sleek and dark,
Who, on a rhododendron bush,
Warbled to a missel-thrush.
He preened and sang unbridled, for
He cared no whit about the war.

No thought of rationing or raid
Occurred to mar his serenade,
And politicians were to him,
I knew, superfluous and grim.
He honed his beak for an encore:
He cared no whit about the war.

F. Tennyson Jesse

is another occasional poet, better known as a novelist. Four lines in 'Testament' indicate that she can steer her way through life without the lamp of religion. She is typical of her period also in her frank acceptance of the body's part in human love, and the three following pieces express a modern attitude toward sex which has not hitherto appeared in these pages. Aphra Behn could be 'daring' or 'naughty', and Laurence Hope startled her own generation by the warm sensuality of the 'Indian Love Lyrics'; but here is a far more delicate sensuousness than we may get from either of the earlier poets.

123 Testament

I will and bequeath
What—and to whom?
There is no child
Of my eager womb.
But if there's thought
Born of experience,
Teaching us lenience,
One should have wrought
Some knowledge to leave
To one who may grieve.
We die and all's over,
Love and the lover,
Fun of food and the sun,
Of the flesh that is one
For a few beating moments,
Of the soul that believes
In the notion of oneness
Ere again it must grieve
In the knowledge of loneness.
We are what we are,
With children or none
Each soul is alone
Under moon or sun.
I will and bequeath—

Well, what did I start with?
Faith, hope and charity,
Youth, beauty, stupidity,
Total lack of cupidity,
No fear, but acceptance
Of life—in priest's vestment;
Gilded, ordered and blest
With a God to invest
One's tiniest movements
With cosmic importance.
I will and bequeath
My faith, hope and charity
To those who can still
Credit such rarity.
Youth, beauty; stupidity
I gave to my lover.
They are all gone
Now that love's over.
He gave in return
Lust, Joy and Security.
I will and bequeath
To those who believe
That there's life in maturity
My lust, joy and security.
I will and bequeath
My God to those fools
Who say in their hearts
There's a God and He rules.
I will and bequeath
My love to my lover
Who'll be able to breathe
When my life is over.

124 Lover's Wish

I would be bread
That you of me might eat;
I would be wine
That I could slake your drouth;

I would be air
To blow as softly sweet
As kisses on your mouth.

Would I were earth
To bear your body up;
Would I were sun
To warm you as you lay,
Or water, I,
To hold you like a cup
Lapping you every way.
Would I could lie
Close, close, within your flesh,
Beat in your pulse,
Brim to your eager eyes,
Burn in your blood—
So, woven in one mesh,
Your breath would be my sighs.

Body and soul
I would be part of you,
No more myself
But you, the heart of you.

125 Lover's Memory

I fold my two hands o'er my face
And in that little shade of night,
A Gothic arch for me alone,
My closed eyes see you standing bright;
While to the memory of my hands
My knowledge of your body gives
Each slope and curve that once I knew,
And in my hands your body lives.

So were I blind, as now I make pretend,
Still would yourself be with me till love's end.

Olga Katzin

is known everywhere under a pseudonym which I must not divulge. Except for the Drydenesque 'Prologue', these poems are very early work and, like several of our contributors, the author has a pronounced distaste for her juvenilia. She might do well to re-read 'The Player Queen'. Years ago that remarkable man-of-letters, Havelock Ellis, perhaps exaggerating a little, observed to me, 'Few men write good poetry after they are forty, and until he is forty no man can write a first-rate novel. His experience may have been intense but it cannot have been varied enough.'

Olga Katzin is of Russian stock and came from South Africa. There is an almost incessant twinkle in her literary eye—but I must not tell where it may be seen.

126 The Romantic

I think the city's iron tide
And all its shapes of clamour, mean
Less than a shadow on a wall,
Because from these my soul can hide
Deep in the woods of dancing green
And hear the hidden cuckoo call.

Or words from half-forgotten tales
Can break this prison, and create
A world as wide, where life goes free;
Where men may spread adventuring sails
For white bird-haunted cliffs that wait
Sun-smitten, in the storied sea.

And though I also fight for bread
Among the hungry, to my way
No part of their poor pain belongs.
For dreaming with the happier dead
I walk enchanted; and all day
My heart is drunken with old songs.

127 The Player Queen

We lie in the King's Hall at Winchester
This Twelfth Night. There's a moon-ray striking down
Across the pillar and the arrassed wall,
Touching with light the cloak of miniver,
The rose-red wimple and long yellow gown
I played Queen Dido in, and there let fall.—

They came with the court minstrels through that door
After the banquet: first, the white-faced Queen,
Then, sideways smiling, very fair, her maid,
And many richly-kirtled ladies more,
With long-haired squires; and last, the prince in green,
With glancing eyes, like his Italian blade.

We played our play. Then, by the throne one stirred,
Dropping a flower; and, like a man asleep,
Spell-chained by love that has so little joy,
The prince bent down; close upon that I heard
Sighing, and thought the Queen was like to weep
But not for Dido, or the prince of Troy.

Her eyes were deeper than a midnight pool;
She went with music. Once was Dido dear
That slew herself for love. Both Queens, and yet
What boots it to be Queen, and sorrowful?
Yonder the huntsmen and Queen Guinevere
Move on the arras. And the moon has set.

128 Prologue

(*Written for the re-opening of the Theatre Royal, Richmond, Yorkshire, 1942.*)

Enter the Spirit of the Theatre.

I vow I won't be gagged, I won't be tied!
No Person ever was so mortified!
A Prisoner in these Walls I've been confined,
And I'll be hanged now, but I'll speak my Mind.

I'm vastly grateful you have set me free
From long, unmerited Captivity,
But can you marvel I'm in such a Huff?
One hundred years of Silence is enough!
These ancient Playbills tell my former Fame,
When Actors of renown to Richmond came,
Great Kemble, and Macready here were seen,
Majestic Siddons, and immortal Kean!
Here first Miss Wallis curtsey'd, Richmond's Boast,
The rage of Bath, and Covent Garden's Toast!
Here Passion stalked, here Comedies of Wit
Brought down the Gods and mesmerised the Pit.
But then the lights went out, and I was left,
Of Actors and of Audience bereft,
Alone in horrid Solitude to freeze
'Mid Dust enough to make a Statue sneeze.
And last O Horror! Infamy! O Shame!
The Minions of the Corporation came,
Flung me to Earth and heaped upon my Lap,
Rags, bones, waste-paper, rubber, metal-scrap,
And 'neath this Mountain stifled long I lay
Nor guessed Deliverance was on the way.
But now once more I snuff the Playhouse Air,
I'm feeling hugely better, I declare!
I warrant you, you'll find me worth my Ransom,
For seen by Candlelight I'm not unhandsome.
And see, my Treasures, guarded all this while
From black Oblivion—and the salvage Pile—
Ophelia's Wreath, and Alexander's Crown,
Othello's Handkerchief, and Prospero's Gown!
(Though you might think it tarnished, mouldy stuff,
Yet, brushed and shaken, 'twill do well enough)
And best of all, these antique, dog-eared Books
From cobwebbed Corners snatch'd by Mr. Brooks.
Lord, I could stand and gossip for an Age
About this Playhouse, this historic Stage!
But there's the Prompter, waving me aside—
Just one Word more; this I'll not be denied.

Let us a Bargain strike before I go—
This is your Theatre, pray keep it so,
And never turn it from its lawful Use
Or me condemn to Silence and Abuse.
I am your Hostage; only let me live
And I will prove I've Something still to give.
Leave me but Life, good Friends, and for my part,
If you will grant me Life, I'll give you Art.
If you consent give me your hands, I pray.
The Prologue is dismissed. Here comes the Play.

Joan Lamburn

This writer of Children's Books (about strange horses and self-respecting cats) is a perpetual twinkler, for even when she is writing of a sad experience she remains aloof and without self-pity. By nature she is so retiring, despite her swift intelligence, that only by accident did my collaborator discover the curiously-carven cherrystones which are now revealed. There is uncommon observation in 'The Celibate': we know the true personality of that man. Only a contemporary could have written the courageous but true couplet which ends 'How will you remember me?' A Victorian would have been tearful.

129 First Cause

I am nothing, so for me
Nothing is a verity.
That nothing comes of nothing may be true,
But only when you nothing do can aught begin
From your own being. It is the endless din
Of doing and undoing as we spin
In space leads men to say they nothing fear.
They do fear nothing—true,
For nothingness to them is death,
But you in whom my spirit lives can sink
Into the nothingness from which they shrink
And be re-born as lightly as a breath.

130 The Celibate

Half-satyr and half-saint, you walk alone,
Haunted by ancient sins you must atone,
Tortured by fiery blood in veins that freeze
At thought of God whose wrath you must appease
Before you are absolved the mortal love
Your mother knew, and bearing you did prove;
For though by Nature's law the world must mate,
All godly men their naturalness must hate!
So do you turn away your saintly head
To see not where your satyr's hooves would tread,
Weaving through woods a path for nymphs to follow—
O tell me, now,—is head or hoof more hollow?

131 Bondage

Must I love again, knowing that love grows cold?
Is my heart to be plundered,
And fresh bonds take the place of the old,
So painfully sundered?
Love is a bondage, a torment, a strife—
All three.
May I love, by God's grace, to the end of my life,
Never free.

132 How will you remember me?

How will you remember me
When our playing's ended?
When you find it cannot be
The masque that you intended.
Dull of tongue and slow of wit,
Still I have one virtue,
When of me you would be quit,
I quickly will desert you.
Others you may like to tease

And many will enchant you,
Alas, in you was all my ease,
And none may now supplant you.
But loving fools have never yet
Gained by remembrance, so—forget.

Eiluned Lewis

Our only Welsh poet (and that is truly strange) achieved prominence with her sensitive account of childhood, 'Dew on the Grass'. The Brute who should 'disdain'

'To share his quiet hearth with Jane'

would deserve complete ostracism; but the thought of him leads us to imagine, as best we can, the kind of verses which Miss Austen might have written. Perhaps they would have been tidy, twinkling, melodious and old-fashioned.

133 Man and his Books

As squirrels store their autumn hoard,
And farmers bind their stooks,
And bees make mead from vagrant blooms,
So man puts by his books.
They will not heed November's breath
These leaves, that nothing know of Death.

And he, their lord, how fortunate!
How splendid his abode
Who views the waves Ulysses sailed,
The land where Quixote rode,
And sees at dusk, 'neath English skies,
The camp fire of Lavengro rise.

With Benvenuto he can quaff
The gleaming Tuscan wine;
Hear Boswell question, Johnson roar,
With Surtees hunt and dine.
A gentleman would ne'er disdain
To share his quiet hearth with Jane.

In such rare company no man
Need ever mope or rust;
He will despise the creeping years,
Forget that he is dust,
And find such richness in his days
That life's too short to sing its praise.

134 The Birthright

We who were born
In country places,
Far from cities
And shifting faces,
We have a birthright
No man can sell
And a secret joy
No man can tell
For we are kindred
To lordly things,
The wild duck's flight
And the white owl's wings;
To pike and salmon,
To bull and horse,
The curlew's cry
And the smell of gorse.

Pride of trees,
Swiftness of streams,
Magic of frost
Have shaped our dreams:
No baser vision
Their spirit fills
Who walk by right
On the naked hills.

Lilian Bowes-Lyon

This poet brings another new mood into this book, and it is interesting to compare her 'Allendale' with Mrs. Browning's 'Flush': poems of strikingly different breed. Dogs have less often been celebrated in verse than cats, possibly because a dog is a pronounced extrovert and most poets have been introverts. The cat, we may say, is The Muses' Pet—from Gray to Swinburne, who addressed one of the species as 'Stately, kindly, lordly friend.'

135 Allendale Dog

A lean tyke, supple
As the long winds that ripple
Counties cool as ivory,
He wills the moving reverie
Of northerly-fathered flocks.
Prick-eared, he lurks
To leeward, patiently bold;
Lift arm or lift an eyebrow,
He'll weave his sky-brow
Spell round the offender
Who has taken leave to wander,
Re-knotting as if by chance
The cordon of Providence.

His fibre of wit is spun
From the careful brain of man,
Yet gleams in its own right;
He skims gay light
From mountains gaunt with cold;
Certain as love, brings home
The blundering ewe, the lamb
By snows in March confounded;
You storm-bound Jill or Jack,
Me too he has befriended.

Fells under heaven are his;
The poet he is
Of dawns that wring new gold
Like dew from danger's fleece,
And the sheep-bell's travelling peace.

Oh comrade emperors lack!

Katherine Mansfield

No one who appreciated the hyper-sensitive observation and psychical awareness in the short stories of Katherine Mansfield will be surprised by 'The Gulf', but some readers may not have anticipated the simple and glowing happiness expressed in the 'Rangitaki' verses.

Technically it is worth noting that so early as 1909 young writers were rebelling against precise metres. They had no wish to endure the scrupulous self-discipline which has conferred immortality on Horace and Pope. Raggéd rhythm, inherited from that great innovator Walt Whitman, becomes almost general with the Edwardians: but if prose turns rancid when its writer slips unintentionally into blank verse, what ought we to think of verse when it is essentially indistinguishable from bad prose? In 'Rangitaki' this has not quite happened, though the verse-pattern is becoming blurred. The translators of the Authorised Version recognised the boundary between prose and verse, for although they found so many memorable poetic phrases they hardly ever over-rhythmicised their superb prose.

136 In the Rangitaki Valley

O valley of waving broom,
O lovely, lovely light,
O heart of the world, red-gold!
Breast high in the blossom I stand;
It beats about me like waves
Of a magical, golden sea.

The barren heart of the world
Alive at the kiss of the sun,
The yellow mantle of Summer
Flung over a laughing land,
Warm with the warmth of her body,
Sweet with the kiss of her breath.

O valley of waving broom,
O lovely, lovely light,
O mystical marriage of Earth
With the passionate Summer sun!
To her lover she holds a cup
And the yellow wine o'erflows.
He has lighted a little torch
And the whole of the world is ablaze.
Prodigal wealth of love!
Breast high in the blossom I stand.

137 The Gulf

A gulf of silence separates us from each other.
I stand at one side of the gulf, you at the other.
I cannot see you or hear you, yet know that you are there.
Often I call you by your childish name
And pretend that the echo to my crying is your voice.
How can we bridge the gulf? Never by speech or touch.
Once I thought we might fill it quite up with tears.
Now I want to shatter it with our laughter.

Ruth Pitter

Few sights are more melancholy than the spectacle of an elderly author frantically trying to keep up with the young, for the truth is that after a certain age everybody finds a new mode in any art disconcerting or unintelligible. Swinburne could see no merit in Yeats. I said 'everybody', but I ought to have excepted Leigh Hunt. There is no poem in Part Five which I do not like or admire, but it would be hypocrisy to pretend that I understand every line of every poem: and it must follow as the night the day that the poets themselves will be perplexed by their followers in, say, 1980.

In much modern verse rhyme is replaced by assonance, a dubious practice because it is surely better to provide pure rhymes or none at all. The reader is likely to agree that Ruth Pitter is a genuine and considerable poet. 'The Tall Fruit Trees' is an interesting example of the degree to which realism has now been blended with poetry. Fifty years ago no poet, unless it were Meredith, would have used the graphic, homely touch—'yet four foot short of the ladder we're needing.' These are the touches that give many persons a feeling that poetry, after all, is not really above their heads. An architect, speaking in 1912, showed that he was delighted by Rupert Brooke's query, 'And will there still be jam for tea?'

There is no need to dilate upon the sincerity of the lines, some of them stoically grim, in the following poems, but it may be worth while to suggest (once more) that the minute observation in 'The Strawberry Plant' would be surprising in a man-poet—even in Tennyson or Browning.

138 If you came

If you came to my secret glade,
   Weary with heat,
I would set you down in the shade,
   I would wash your feet.

If you came in the winter sad,
   Wanting for bread,
I would give you the last that I had,
   I would give you my bed.

But the place is hidden apart
   Like a nest by a brook,
And I will not show you my heart
   By a word, by a look.

The place is hidden apart
  Like the nest of a bird:
And I will not show you my heart
  By a look, by a word.

139—1938

O when will they let them love
As they are dying to do,
Men, creatures, brave spirits, friends,
The flower and the wonder of life?
They weep and die, and their bones
Mingle in earth, as never
In life could their aching minds,
Lost and parted, betrayed and forsaken!

They are shreds of a garment of gold
Flapping from many a thorn;
The sharp-edged fragments of a great vessel
That should be holding the wine;
The stones of a princely house,
Showing each some feature of grace,
But broken and scattered asunder,
The mortar being perished.

The greatest harvests of time—
Abundance, if fairly divided—
Are burned or thrown in the sea:
The mind, with its burden of love
Corrupting, now heavily weighs
The means of a myriad deaths.

The gentle are ground into earth
And the tender despised:
Honour's an ass-head, a bauble,
The mark of a profitless fool;
The good man's goal is the grave,
His secret longing extinction.

The numberless warring voices
There keep unanimous silence,
The minds that conceived the slaughter
Are merged in harmless oblivion,
The hand that snatched up the weapon
Lies still, forgetting unkindness.

If only the grave can calm us:
If there my bones and my brother's
Lying in peace, united,
Bring no reproach on the mother
Nor stir the father to anger:

Let us go down together,
Having despaired of wisdom:
The earth is as fruitful as ever,
The sea still teeming with fishes,
The sun still lusty; but we
Have failed to love, and must perish.

140 The Strawberry Plant

Above the water, in her rocky niche,
She sat enthroned and perfect; for her crown
One bud, like pearl, and then two fairy roses
Blanched and yet ardent in their flowing hearts;
One greenish berry spangling into yellow
Where the light touched the seed: one fruit achieved
And ripe, an odorous vermillion ball
Tight with completion, lovingly enclasped
By the close cup whose green chimed with the red,
And showered with drops of gold like Danae:
Three lovely sister leaves as like as peas,
Young but full-fledged, dark, with a little down:
Two leaves that to a matron hue inclined;
And one the matriarch, that dressed in gold
And flushed with wine, thought her last days her best.

And here and there a diamond of dew
Beamed coolly from the white, smiled from the gold,
Silvered the down, struck lightning from the red.
The overhanging rock forbade the sun,
Yet was she all alight with water-gleams
Reflected, like the footlights at a play:
Perfection's self, and (rightly) out of reach.

141 The Tall Fruit Trees

I'll lop them, it will be easier so to tend them;
Then we may clean them, and gather the fruit with ease
No one can do with these great old orchard trees,
Dirty, shady, unwieldy—don't try to defend them.

O promise to do them one or two at a time then—
That will make you twenty years in going the rounds:
Then the tall tops for me will be out of bounds,
Surely I shall no longer be able to climb then.

But while I am able O let me ascend the plum-tree
And poke my head out at the top, where the lovely view
Has a foreground of scarlet plums with a wash of blue,
And I am away from earth in the starlings' country.

And for a few years yet spend a day in the pear-tree,
Squirming and stretching, plagued by the wasps and the twigs,
Scratches all over me, bruised in the arms and legs,
Coming down whacked at last from the great old bare tree—

And yet not wholly bare, for his topmost steeple
Still flaunts a fair wreath of a dozen, the best of all;
Ha, he beat me at last, for he was so tall—
He will not give his best work up to greedy people.

And there is the huge gaunt apple-tree, dead man's seedling,
With five great limbs, spreading twenty feet from the ground;
How he makes us stagger the longest ladder around,
So heavy—yet four foot short of the ladder we're needing.

Some years he's good for bushels of small red apples
  That keep well enough, and roast well enough by the fire,
But every year he is young and brave with desire,
  Smothered in rosy wreaths that the sunlight dapples.

Dappled with sunlight and bright with the Maytime raindrop,
  Mighty from age and youthful with tender bloom,
He heaves up brightness and scent to our highest room,
  Brushes the dormer-window with shining maintop.

We'll take in a bit more ground, and plant it with limber
  Maidens on dwarfing stocks, at twelve feet apart;
But the great old trees are the real loves of my heart,
  Mountains of blossom and fruit on the stalwart timber.

Kathleen Raine

It is easy to detect that this writer is fortunate enough to have a sustaining religious faith. Like Wrenne Jarman, she has been severely troubled by the miseries of war, as we find in 'Mourning in Spring, 1943'. Her latest book (1946) contains an outstandingly splendid poem about womanhood ('The Goddess') with the lines:

> 'House of gold, palace of ivory,
>   Gate of heaven and rose of mystery.'

She is also a subtle critic and a writer of firm prose.

142 Heroes

This war's dead heroes, who has seen them?
They rise in smoke above the burning city,
Faint clouds, dissolving into sky.

And who sifting the Libyan sand can find
The tracery of a human hand,
The faint impression of an absent mind,
The fade-out of a soldier's day dream?

You'll know your love no more, nor his sweet kisses—
He's forgotten you, girl, and in the idle sun
In long green grass that the east wind caresses
The seed of man is ravished by the corn.

143 Mourning in Spring, 1943

O you girls, girl friends, you who have also loved
The fertile gods Osiris, and Adonis
Whose garden has flowered for centuries from our blood,
Though love was different for each of us,
Know now, he is dying, our lover, dying all over the world.

Dying all over the world—his death will stain
The green fields crimson, extinguish the bright south,
Make the north frigid for ever, embitter the ocean,
Make the east to the west, his funeral blackens the sun's path.

These were our men, whose destiny is the desert,
And those who were last seen struggling in the sea,
Though not for long—the waves now have washed them away
And their ears and mouths and hearts are muted with sand.

These were our men—now nameless among death's millions,
Our sons, our darlings that we have cherished from the world's creation,
These were the lovers that wiped all tears from our eyes,
And now our sterile wombs and broken hearts
Are the measure of war's disaster, and love's price.

144 The Rose

What does the eye see?
A rose-bed on a paradise tree.

What does hope say?
A rose shall fill time with eternity!

What is memory's refrain?
'I was that rose before the world began.'

What does thought foretell?
Petal upon petal,
World within world, star within cell.

What sings love then?
'I am the rose, that crimson rose is mine.'

Why comes death this way?
To take away, to take my rose away.

What lies in the immortal centre hidden?
Mary on the golden throne of Heaven.

And in the heart of Heaven what lives, what grows?
The heart of Heaven is the rose, the rose.

Irene Rathbone

'Was there a Summer?' is, by modern standards, a long poem. It describes an impermanent but enriching love-experience. It might be regarded as a 'companion-piece' to Richard Aldington's no less beautiful 'A Dream in the Luxembourg'. Extracts can offer only a weak taste of the author's high-hearted poem. We give merely the opening and ending, but recommend the reader to find out the entire work. He or she will be richly rewarded.

145 *From:* "Was there a Summer?"

I had loved him for a year
(If that can be called love
Which only knows the mind of a man
His mind through his books)
Had loved him with such delighted certainty
That I wrote him letters:
The letters were not sent—save one.
They lay in piles, quivering with their own life,
In my desk.
At the end of the year I sent him one;

I said 'This poem of yours which has just appeared . . .'
I said . . . It doesn't matter.
I tried to be coolly restrained,
Just an appreciative member of the public
Writing to an author about his poem.
But I knew (though he had never seen me)
I knew that that poem had been written for me.
Yes, though the trees in Kensington Gardens
Shrug tired shoulders,
Though the mist lies blue beneath their rounded tolerant shoulders
I knew that this was my poem.
And I knew (oh, indifferent London)
That this was my man.
It is hard to sit here and write,
Remembering those days;
Hard to sit on a small green chair
('Tuppence please lady')
And see myself one of that timeless stream of women
Who, from Œnone downwards,
(The fat man on the next chair is reading in the *Evening Standard*
Of a typist who gassed herself)
From Œnone downwards
Have believed the words of men
And been deserted.
Hard; but I mean to do it, for forgetfulness is death—
Or for that matter death forgetfulness—
(See *Evening Standard*: Typist's Last Letter)
And I want neither.

So fade out, London trees!
Fade, fur-wrapped ladies
Hurrying with small reluctant dogs back down dim paths
To teas in Kensington,
Fade . . .
And shine Provence!

I have been blind with pain
But then

Blind almost with bliss too;
And it is a thing to accept
That the men who are the joy-bringers
Are inevitably the grief bringers.
It is not their fault.
Why should I call him faithless
Because his wings are not pinioned?
Because others besides myself are sung to?
Others besides myself are taken
With him on wheeling flights through the enchanted air?
We know what Blake says:
We know that wingéd joys die if imprisoned;
I have been given a desperate strength
Not to reach hands at mine.
Yes, and if that self in me—that other who bleeds—cries
Songless your life now
Starless and fooled you go
I shall not say it's a falsehood;
Only
Only that its opposite is also true.

And now lamps wink at the end of vistas,
And months ago the fat man on the next chair
Went home, leaving his *Evening Standard*.
I must pick up my dispatch-case
And hurry on sensible feet down the path,
A path which doesn't lie beneath pine trees
And isn't sandy
But gray and made of asphalt
With fallen leaves on it,
And it leads
Out at iron railings
Into the muffled roar
Of what is known as
Reality.

Phyllis Reid

is principally a love-poet, and has written an admirable group of love sonnets. Here, in fact, is a specialist in the sonnet (as also in the vilanelle), one who manifestly delights in circumscribed forms. And yet in 'Fireworks' we have another semi-realistic impression, and in 'Wind' an example of the lyrical expression of sheer youthful high-spirits which is rare in our poetry. Her work is at present (1947) not published in book form. She has always wavered between the traditional and the rebellious. Not many living poets have so delicate an 'ear', and this may partly be due to her training in the delivery of verse at the Central School of Dramatic Art and Speech-Training, under the exacting supervision of the late Elsie Fogerty.

146 Naked and alone

Child born in the cawl,
  Suddenly crying
When the torrents of bright air
  Pour over him—his birth
  Is dying. Crying
  To greet life—and again
To leave it—crying . . .

Naked and alone I came,
  Spun my strange cocoon,
Lived and loved here, with a name
  As others have, and soon
I shall go
  Naked and alone.

147 A Song of Green

Moist and soft and crinkled like a baby's fingers
Are the youngest beechleaves of the spring;
When the sunlight slants through them,
When a stirring wind lifts them—
You look upon a gentle lovely thing.

They are so cool, so quiet,
You catch your breath in wonder
That Earth's imagination, in such unsullied joy,
Has made for you another Song of Innocence, as holy
As ever were the poet's lamb or happy shepherd boy.

148 Fireworks

(Reflections after November 5th)

Long ago, November
Was lit by fireworks, and I remember
Still, the thrill of spending three long-hoarded shillings
In a little shop that used to sell only stationery.
The week before the fifth—behold
A magic change
Would enfold it. The window was bright
With coloured sticks and gaily paper-flowered Roman candles,
And tight crinkled crackers.
And there was a smell inside—
The sharp perilous smell of gunpowder—
How to decide
The best outlay of three shillings? . . .
We must have rockets, of course, and again
Golden Rain was safer than Catherine Wheels,
(These sometimes refused to turn, wouldn't burn,
If the nail was too close to the ladder-end holding them.)
But always the crackers—
(Backarappers they were called)
Meant the fearful joy of jumping aside, as they sprang
Zig-zag after girl, after boy—
Oh, fireworks were fun!
And the mystery of the dank dark garden, unlit
Till the sudden flare of a squib
Showed the mysterious boxes where
Fairy fires waited—we had to be brave
To save squibs to the very end, they would bend,
Nearly (but seldom quite) burning our fingers.

The dark-light pattern lingers
Making an unforgettable design
On a child's heart—that was November.

Will children ever again love fireworks?
November colours remain,
Red poppies for Armistice Day,
Red ruin of war—but no more
The gay gunpowder toys. A glare
Sinister instead
Tinges the air overhead.
I shall never hear
Even in a peaceful year
The rocket's swift swishing sigh falling,
Without recalling those seconds of time
Before the bombs landed—never again
The coloured stars, the Golden Rain
Will mean anything but enemy flares
Lighting our land to death.
The pattering rat-tat-tatting of the crackers
Are sticks of incendiaries,
Their mutter on pavement, in gutter—
And the sparkling Catherine Wheel
Becomes a martyrdom of more
Than a saint of yore—
Fireworks are fun
No longer. November's feast is over and done.

November 1942.

149 Wind

This is a giant day—
Run out and pick a tree,
Seize a great flaring beech
And wave it overhead.
Run shouting through the fields,
Leap hedges and rivers,
Maenads will spring to meet you,

Contesting the race.
Run—though you trail the clouds,
Run through the roaring world,
This is a giant day.

150 Sonnet

As a seed deeply sheathed within a cone,
I dream I lie close-folded in your heart,
Of its strange structure I become a part,
A life not living to itself alone.
Through you into fair fruit I might have grown,
Yourself transmuted by the tender art
You used to make a lovely counterpart
Of what you held intrinsically your own.

I dream—a great wind shakes me to the ground—
Waking, my love grows not on any tree
God planted in the forests of the earth.
Separate you grew, and separately have found
Fruition. Well, your friending love is worth
If not my dream, my waking life to me.

151 Sonnet

As one who lingers over some old store
Of faded treasures, hoping to ensnare
The spirit of a love that once dwelt there
And life out of the fragrant dust restore,
Finds memory, that has not any more
The heart of being, but in the living air
Crumbles to nothingness—so do I fare
Who seek for friendship at dead passion's door.

All that was beautiful, all that was good
Between us, now should sweeten and control;
And yet our words like dead leaves round us fall,
Your eyes still smile, yet are not eyes at all;
Meeting that's heartache I had understood,
But not, ah not this blankness of the soul.

152 Sonnet

Do not be angry with me for the word
Left unfulfilled after such hesitation,
Cry not upon our summer's desecration,
Sweet ways untrod, the lark's high song unheard.
Passion's deep pool we passed, strangely deterred,
Skirting the margin, lest the perturbation
Of just one pebble flung in jubilation
In rippling rings the surface might have stirred.

Ah, we have played with life and we must pay
With sharpened knowledge of delight foregone.
The young shoots died ere they had time to grow,
And my hand bruised them; but I dare not say
Yours might have saved—The summer lingers on
Wasted; for what? My dear, I do not know.

Anne Ridler

Here is a poet whose work is a marked example of the modern tendency to avoid being continuously poetical. Not only does she introduce touches of realism which would have astonished a Victorian reader ('the chimney that over Lords looms'), but also uses lines which, taken out of their context, could hardly be more prosaic: for instance, 'Lying in a tight occipital position' and 'what immunity we have from the germ of the printed lie.' From the days of Hesiod and Virgil, poets have always used a considerable measure of realism in describing country matters, and this must be because the phenomena of country life are unchanging. Some fifty years ago the German poet Richard Dehmel wrote of 'the telegraph wires moaning', and one of our more recent poets has written about 'pylons'. The danger of using urban or scientific realism in poetry arises from the fact that the objects described may have merely a temporary interest. The value of mixing prosaic with poetic phrases may be, like the use of occasional dissonance in fairly modern music, that they preclude a cloying sweetness, but the danger comes from the risk of altogether destroying a poetic emotion. Anne Ridler is a meditative rather than a lyric poet, and presumably does not aim at a lyrical effect.

153 For a Christening

Meditation and Invocation

I

In June the early signs,
And after, the steady labour of subcutaneous growth:
Past the danger of dissolution in the third month,
And in the fifth, quickens.
But hidden while the leaves thicken, through the season when smooth corn
Grows bearded, through the peeling of the summer's gold fleece;
Hidden but with heart throbbing, while stars sharpen and throb in the skies,
While sunsets grow cold and orange, while winter airs are whirled and torn;
And at Candlemas with pain is born.
Lying with a right occipital position, what prompts it we may never know,
But at the appointed time dives down, down into the light—
Blinding snow-light, piercing the darkest corner with white,
Brightness of prick-eared cyclamen pink against the snow—
So long hidden, so sudden into sight.

II

You are our darling and our foreign guest;
We know all your origins, and this is to know nothing.
Distinguished stranger to whom we offer food and rest;
Yet made of our own natures; yet looked for with such longing.
Helpless wandering hands, the miniature of mine,
Fine skin and furious look and little raging voice,—
Your looks are full human, your qualities all hidden:
It is your mere existence we have by heart, and rejoice.

The wide waters of wonder and comprehension pour
Through this narrow weir, and irresistible their power.
The rainbow multiple glory of our humanity cannot pierce
As does the single white beam of your being.
This makes your presence so shattering a grace,
Unsheathed suddenly from the womb: it was none of our intending
To set in train a miracle; and yet it is merely
Made palpable in you, missed elsewhere by diffusion.
Therefore we adore God-in-our-flesh as a baby:
Whose Being is his Essence, and outside It, illusion.
Later, the fulfilment, the example, death, misprision—
Here the extraordinary fact of Being, which we see
Stripped and simple as the speechless stranger on my knee.

III

Blessing, sleep and grow taller in sleeping.
Lie ever in kind keeping.
Infants curl in a cowrie of peace
And should lie lazy. After this ease,
When the soul out of its safe shell goes,
Stretched as you stretch those knees and toes,
What should I wish you? Intelligence first,
In a credulous age by instruction cursed.
Take from us both what immunity
We have from the germ of the printed lie.
Your father's calm temper I wish you, and
The shaping power of his confident hand.
Much, too, that is different and your own;
And may we learn to leave you alone.
For your part, forgive us the pain of living,
Grow in that harsh sun great-hearted and loving.

Sleep, little honey, then; sleep while the powers
Of the Nine Bright Shiners[1] and the Seven Stars

[1] See 'Green Grow the Rashes O', *English County Songs*, ed. Lucy Broadwood, where a note explains that in one English interpretation, as in the Hebrew version, it refers to the nine months preceding birth.

Harmless, encircle: the natural world
Lifegiving, neutral, unless despoiled
By our greed or scorn. And wherever you sleep—
My arms outgrown—or waking weep,
Life is your lot: you lie in God's hand,
In his terrible mercy, world without end.

154 In Regent's Park

These Sunday mornings Londoners delight—
with or without the trotting child—
their workday eyes grown mild
but with their panoply precise and spry,
the handsome pleasure-ways of parks to try.

Dahlias down the banks flow crisp and bright,
the grass is winter-short and pungent,
dipping oars are plangent,
and in the light mist, dripping grey like silk,
water and trees and air seem smoothed in milk.

So that the forbidden island in the stream,
the chimney that over Lords looms,
and those peculiar domes,
might be near or distant illimitable miles;
and as the still sky breaks into a thousand gulls,

might burst into some bright or strange kind,
or open into a different scale.
To change in this style
is the property, I find, of love, which brings
a new dimension to all physical things.

For if I see my park with Vivian's eye—
the formal eye of a painter's mind—
it is changed as under his hand,
and through the mists of his being are visible
hints of glory before unimaginable.

One does not learn to look with another's eye
  for ever, but the rigid world
moves and is unfurled.
This is the effect and virtue of passion's part,
that trains the eye and exercises the heart.

Joyce Rowe

As a direct descendant of Nicholas Rowe, the Poet Laureate who was among the earliest editors of Shakespeare, this young writer is remotely connected with Elizabeth Rowe (p. 27). She is definitely a 'singer', a lyric-poet, a belated troubadour who enjoys jingling the golden rhymes in her wallet. There is much of April and 'the sweet o' the year' in her verse, and at times she will kick up her heels like a Spring-inspired tomboy; but most of her work at present is war-troubled.

155 Past Song

This is the lean year yet green year of my giving.
This is the first time and the worst time of my living.
Yet the fire burns and the world turns away
And yesterday prepares to face to-day.
I, like to-morrow, shuffle in my queue,
But you, beloved, what is this to you?

I had nothing and to nothing have returned.

This is the only lesson I have learned
And all my tunes revert to this refrain
With scattered notes of ecstasy and pain. . . .
The past song—the last song—I shall not sing again.

I had nothing and to nothing have returned.

How long ago since harassed Paris spurned
Power and silver for a woman's curving thigh?
Her way of walking or her laughing eye?

Those days are dead like all the tales they told—
Love's molten metal in convention's mould
Grows cooler, cooler and, at long last, cold.

I nothing had, to nothing have returned.

This was the only lesson to be learned
Through unimagined bliss, exceeding pain,
Dear past song—my last song—I shall not sing again.

156 Without Syncopation

O, for that long littleness. We only know
the brief extravagance of a kiss,
the stab of wonder and the spear's twist.
Knowledge grows as trees throw out their leaves,
as children chase balloons, adults their satisfaction.
And knowledge asks for action.
So do we turn and turn about,
stamping alleged adventurous feet
on the same well-trod spot.
Fling out
your shoots, so piercing sweet,
pale eerie snowdrops, through the ground,
that self-same ground on which we beat
monotony, bound in our own staccato circles.
We have not wit enough to see that spring
reiterates the same enchanting thing
with fair variety.
That yearly miracle, too rare for touch,
too quietly commonplace for us
who think we know so much.

Margot Ruddock

W. B. Yeats wrote of Margot Ruddock:

'Meanwhile I had discovered her poetry. She sent me passionate incoherent improvizations. . . . I criticised her with some vehemence and the improvizations became coherent poems. . . . Here in broken sentences, in ejaculations, in fragments of all kinds was a power of expression of spiritual suffering unique in her generation.'

157 I Take Thee, Life

I take thee, Life,
Because I need,
A wanton love
My flesh to feed.

But still my soul
Insatiate
Cries out, cries out
For its true mate.

Victoria Sackville-West

Any group of poetry lovers might reasonably consider the proposition that Victoria Sackville-West is the most notable poet (of either sex) who is now writing in English. Her style is as careful and as aristocratic as that of Gray; her 'ear' is faultless; her workmanship is invariably fine; and the tempo of her verse is noticeably *adagio*. The prevailing mood of her work is a blend of melancholy and stoicism, and both qualities seem to come from a belief that we are not immortal souls but 'perambulating dust'.

Her long poems, 'The Land' (which first brought her into prominence) and 'The Garden', proclaim her as a country-poet but certainly not as a week-end visitor. The gravity of her thought and the nobility of her style remove her as far from the 'horse-and-hound' type of woman as from the status of Landor's 'Little Dainty Poet'.

The first of these poems refers to the old castle in Kent which is now the poet's home.

158 Sissinghurst

A tired swimmer in the waves of time
I throw my hands up: let the surface close:
Sink down through centuries to another clime,
And buried find the castle and the rose.
Buried in time and sleep,
So drowsy, so overgrown,
That here the moss is green upon the stone,
And lichen stains the keep.
I've sunk into an image, water-drowned,
Where stirs no wind and penetrates no sound,
Illusive, fragile to a touch, remote,
Foundered within the well of years as deep
As in the waters of a stagnant moat.
Yet in and out of these decaying halls
I move, and not a ripple, not a quiver,
Shakes the reflection though the waters shiver,—
My tread is to the same illusion bound.
Here, tall and damask as a summer flower,
Rise the brick gables and the spring tower;
Invading Nature crawls
With ivied fingers over rosy walls,
Searching the crevices,
Clasping the mullion, riveting the crack,
Binding the fabric crumbling to attack,
And questing feelers of the wandering fronds
Grope for interstices,
Holding this myth together under-seas,
Anachronistic vagabonds!

And here, by birthright far from present fashion,
As no disturber of the mirrored trance
I move, and to the world above the waters
Wave my incognisance.

For here, where days and years have lost their number,
I let a plummet down in lieu of date,
And lose myself within a slumber
Submerged, elate.

For now the apple ripens, now the hop,
And now the clover, now the barley-crop;
Spokes bound upon a wheel forever turning,
Wherewith I turn, no present manner learning;
Cry neither 'Speed your processes!' nor 'Stop!'
I am content to leave the world awry
(Busy with politic perplexity,)
If still the cart-horse at the fall of day
Clumps up the lane to stable and to hay,
And tired men go home from the immense
                    Labour and life's expense
That force the harsh recalcitrant waste to yield
Corn and not nettles in the harvest-field;
This husbandry, this castle, and this I
                    Moving within the deeps,
Shall be content within our timeless spell,
Assembled fragments of an age gone by,
While still the sower sows, the reaper reaps,
Beneath the snowy mountains of the sky,
And meadows dimple to the village bell.
So plods the stallion up my evening lane
And fills me with a mindless deep repose,
                    Wherein I find in chain
The castle, and the pasture, and the rose.

Beauty, and use, and beauty once again
Link up my scattered heart, and shape a scheme
Commensurate with a frustrated dream.

The autumn bonfire smokes across the woods
And reddens in the water of the moat;
As red within the water burns the scythe,
And the moon dwindled to her gibbous tithe
                    Follows the sunken sun afloat.
Green is the eastern sky and red the west;
The hop-kilns huddle under pallid hoods;
The waggon stupid stands with upright shaft,
As daily life accepts the night's arrest.

Night like a deeper sea engulfs the land,
The castle, and the meadows, and the farm;
Only the baying watch-dog looks for harm,
And shakes his chain towards the lunar brand.
In the high room where tall the shadows tilt
As candle-flames blow crooked in the draught,
The reddened sunset on the panes was spilt,
But now as black as any nomad's tent
The night-time and the night of time have blent
Their darkness, and the waters doubly sleep.
Over my head the years and centuries sweep,
The years of childhood flown,
The centuries unknown;
I dream; I do not weep.

Just as Gibbon's massive style was essential to a history of Rome, so in 'The Bull' we see the writer appropriately composing in paragraphs rather than in detachable lines. Here is a poem which will gain in effect by the minutest examination.

159 The Bull

Now sinks another day to rest
On summer and her leafy ways.
By the last golden light caressed
The farmstead drowses in the haze
Of slanting light in rungs and reins
From heaven slung across the Weald
Above the pricking of the vanes,
More golden than the ripening field
Within the hedgerow squares ensealed.

The owl with short and silent stroke
Deadly to field-fare or to mouse,
Slants from the apple to the oak
Across the orchard near the house;

And through the grasses creep the small
Creatures of twilight, hid by day;
The snail beside the garden wall,
The mole on his myopic way.

The kindly trees protective stand
Around the farm less old than they,
And drawl their shadows on a land
Tilled by a man's forgotten hand,
But still beneath his grandson's sway;
And silent as an empty fane
The barn with doors flung wide
Drinks in the rays of golden rain
On ropes and pulleys, sacks of grain,
A summer evening's pride.

The vanes upon the oasts outside
Have turned their chimneys to the east,
And dim within the shadows deep
Where velvet silence shrouds the roof,
The barn is darkened and asleep.
But in the stall the monstrous beast
Ranges, and stamps a fretful hoof.

The granaries once more are full,
—Oh sweet monotony of the year!—
But in the stall the aging bull
Feels that the end of time is near;
End of that time which was his span,
When he could lash his tail, or browse
On acres all his own,
Or stand four-square and lordly scan
His grass, his calves, his willing cows,
Male, arrogant, alone.
No bachelor! the lord and sire
Of cows and calves in half a shire,
Sole sovereign of his clan;

Whom no man dared approach but he
Who brought the bucket filled with milk,
When little bulls are weak of knee
And muzzled sleek as silk;
Days when within a neighbouring byre
His mother softly mourned her loss,
But he already scampered free
In right and callow disregard,
And kicked his heels, and tried to toss
The empty bucket round the yard.

Days of a lost and youthful spring
Before his liberty was scarred
And branded by the shameful ring;
But what's a ring, when thews are hard
And sex supreme in strength and youth?
A small and negligible thing!

But now resigned within the shed
He moves uneasy round the stall,
And lowers his great tufted head
Against the manger and the wall;
Too patient now for mighty rage,
Too mild and cumbrous and uncouth,
He watches night creep on like age,
And only dimly knows the truth.

The night creeps on; the single star
Of contemplation's lidless eye
Stares through the stable door ajar,
Constant, dispassionate, and high;
Returning at the punctual hour
To stare on man and beast alike,
On rising strength or fallen power,
Nor merciless, nor pitiful,
Without compassion or dislike;
And sees the old and lonely bull
Who does not know that he must die.

The first of the next two poems, a Rembrandtesque 'Interior', might possibly have come from the Lost Books of Jane. The second, with its beautiful last lines, will rejoice any reader who, like Dr. Johnson, appreciates exactitude of speech and abhors a loose phrase.

160 Sometimes When Night . . .

Sometimes when night has thickened on the woods,
And we in the house's square security
Read, speak a little, read again,
Read life at second-hand, speak of small things,
Being content and withdrawn for a little hour
From the dangers and fears that are either wholly absent
Or wholly invading,—sometimes a shot rings out,
Sudden and sharp; complete. It has no sequel,
No sequel for us, only the sudden crack
Breaking a silence followed by a silence,
Too slight a thing for comment; slight, and usual,
A shot in the dark, fired by a hand unseen
At a life unknown; finding, or missing, the mark?
Bringing death? bringing hurt? teaching, perhaps, escape,
Escape from a present threat, a threat recurrent,
Or ending, once and for all? But we read on,
Since the shot was not at our hearts, since the mark was not
Your heart or mine, not this time, my companion.

161 Evening

When little lights in little ports come out,
Quivering down through water with the stars,
And all the fishing fleet of slender spars
Range at their moorings, veer with tide about;

When race of wind is stilled and sails are furled,
And underneath our single riding-light
The curve of black-ribbed deck gleams palely white,
And slumbrous waters pool a slumbrous world,

—Then, and then only, have I thought how sweet
Old age might sink upon a windy youth,
Quiet beneath the riding-light of truth,
Weathered through storms, and gracious in retreat.

The following stanzas are extracted from a poem called 'King's Daughter'.

162 (The Greater Cats)

The greater cats with golden eyes
Stare out between the bars.
Deserts are there, and different skies,
And night with different stars.
They prowl the aromatic hill,
And mate as fiercely as they kill,
And hold the freedom of their will
To roam, to live, to drink their fill;
But this beyond their wit know I:
Man loves a little, and for long shall die.

Their kind across the desert range
Where tulips spring from stones,
Not knowing they will suffer change
Or vultures pick their bones.
Their strength's eternal in their sight,
They rule the terror of the night,
They overtake the deer in flight,
And in their arrogance they smite;
But I am sage, if they are strong:
Man's love is transient as his death is long.

Yet Oh what powers to deceive!
My wit is turned to faith,
And at this moment I believe
In love, and scout at death.
I came from nowhere, and shall be
Strong, steadfast, swift, eternally:

I am a lion, a stone, a tree,
And as the Polar star in me
Is fixed my constant heart on thee.
Ah, may I stay forever blind
With lions, tigers, leopards, and their kind.

Finally we have a delightful *jeu-d'ésprit* which will surprise anybody who fancies that a major poet is always grave: and an early Sonnet which is included 'under protest' from the Poet.

163 Full Moon

She was wearing the coral taffeta trousers
Someone had brought her from Isfahan,
And the little gold coat with pomegranate blossoms,
And the coral-hafted feather fan;
But she ran down a Kentish lane in the moonlight,
And skipped in the pool of the moon as she ran.

She cared not a rap for all the big planets,
For Betelgeuse or Aldebaran,
And all the big planets cared nothing for her,
That small impertinent charlatan,
As she climbed on a Kentish stile in the moonlight,
And laughed at the sky through the sticks of her fan.

164 Early Love

No eye shall see the poem that I write
For you; not even yours; but after long
Forgetful years have passed on our delight
Some hand may chance upon a dusty song
Of those fond days when every spoken word
Was sweet, and all the fleeting things unspoken
Yet sweeter, and the music half unheard
Murmured through forests as a charm unbroken.

Merely the plain and ordinary page
Of two who loved, sole-spirited and clear.
Will you, O stranger of another age,
Not grant a human and compassionate tear
To us, who each the other held so dear?
A single tear fraternal, sadly shed,
Since that which was so living, is so dead.

E. J. Scovell

is a poet who has been praised (in a recent review) by Victoria Sackville-West, but I do not recall whether the elder poet drew special attention to this Tanagra-group of the two sisters. The metre will come refreshingly after so many verses which are either decasyllabic or in no set mould.

165 A Girl to Her Sister

A girl said to her sister, late, when their friends had gone:
'I wish there were no men on earth, but we alone.

'The beauty of your body, the beauty of your face—
Which now are greedy flames, and clasp more than themselves in light,
Pierce awake the drowsing air and boast before the night—
Then should be of less account than a dark reed's grace,
All summer growing in river mists, unknown—
The beauty of your body, the beauty of my own.

'When we two talk together, the words between us pass
Across long fields, across drenched, upland fields of grass,
Like words of men who signal with flags in clear weather.
When we two are together, I know before you speak
Your answers by your head's turn and shadows on your cheek—
Running of wind on grass, to bring our thoughts together.

'We should live as though all day were the day's first hour,
All light were the first daylight, that whistles from so far,
That stills the blood with distance. We should live as though
All seasons were the earliest spring when only birds are mating,

When the low, crouched bramble remembers still the snow
And woods are but half unchained from the winter's waiting.
We should be gay together, with pleasures primrose-cool,
Scattered and quick as spring's are, by thicket and chill pool.

'Oh, to-night,' the girl said, 'I wish that I could sit
All my life here with you, for ever unlit.
To-morrow I shall love again the summer's valour,
Heavy heat of noon, and the night's mysteries,
And love like the sun's touch, that closes up my eyes—
To-morrow; but to-night,' she said, as night ran on,
'I wish there were no love on earth but ours alone.'

Stevie Smith

It will be a calamity if time or journalism or success impairs the unaffected originality of Stevie Smith. At present she can no more be commonplace than a cactus flower can ape a lobelia. Her odd lines, with their impudent disregard of all traditional 'poesy', easily sing themselves into a reader's memory; but under her amusing idiom we see once again a poet who can courageously accept the disappointments of life and its sorrow. May Stevie Smith (as a writer) never be tamed. . . .

166 Le Désert de l'Amour

I want to be your pinkie,
I am tender to you,
My heart opens like a cactus flower,
Do you thinky I will do?

My heart is like a cactus,
Not like a cactus flower,
And I can kill love,
Without entering her bower.

So they both thought. But he was silent and she said:
I cannot see which way you are pointing, the sky is so dark red,
And when the sandstorm is over I will lie down on my bed.

167 The Deathly Child

The deathly child is very gay,
He walks in the sunshine but no shadow falls his way,
He has come to warn us that one must go who would rather stay.

O deathly child
With a heart of woe
And a smile on your face
Who is it that must go?

He walks down the avenue, the trees
Have leaves that are silver when they are turned upon the breeze.
He is more pale than the silver leaves more pale than these.

He walks delicately,
He has a delicate tread.
Why look, he leaves no mark at all
Where the dust is spread.

Over the café tables the talk is going to and fro,
And the people smile and they frown, but they do not know
That the deathly child walks. Ah who is it that must go?

168 The Ghost

'Tis the voice of the Wanderer
I heard her complain
You have weaned me too soon
You must nurse me again
She taps as she passes at each windowpane
Does she not know that she taps in vain?

Her voice flies away on the midnight wind
But would she be happier if she were within?
She is happier far where the night winds fall
And there are no doors and no windows at all.

No man has seen her, this pitiful ghost,
And no woman either, but heard her at most,
Crying and tapping and crying again,
You have weaned me too soon
You must nurse me again.

169 God Speaks to the Man in Despair

Man is my darling, my love and my pain,
My pleasure, my excitement, and my love again,
My wisdom, my courage, my power, my all,
Oh man, do not come to me until I call.

In man is my life, and in man is my death,
He is my hazard, my pride and my breath,
I sought him, I wrought him, I pant on his worth,
In him I experience indeterminate growth.

Oh man, man, of all my animals dearest,
Do not come till I call, though thou weariest first.

170 Touch and Go

Man is coming out of the mountains,
But his tail is caught in the pass,
Why does he not free himself,
Is he not an ass?

Do not be impatient with him,
He is bowed with passion and fret,
He is not out of the mountains,
He is not half out yet.

Look at his sorrowful face,
His torn cheeks, his brow,
He lies with his head in the dust,
Is there no one to help him now?

No, there is no one to help him,
Let him get on with it,
Cry the ancient enemies of Man,
As they cough and spit.

The enemies of man are like trees,
They stand with the sun in their branches,
Is there no one to help my creature,
Where he languishes?

Ah, the delicate creature,
He lies with his head in the rubble,
Pray that the moment pass,
And the trouble.

Look he moves, that is more than a prayer,
But he is so slow,
Will he come out of the mountains?
It is touch and go.

Helen Spalding

This volume contains a number of strange poems but none more strange than 'The Dream'. Ernest Rhys once remarked, 'I thank God I can detect the pedigree of any poem.' He might well have failed to name the literary influences in the piece that follows.

171 The Dream

That evening, when the fire was lit,
She threw a cushion on the floor
Beside his chair; she liked to sit
There at his feet.

'I had a dream last night,' she said,
Gazing into the friendly fire.
'I stood outside a certain door
Knowing that I would come to harm.

I slowly opened it, and saw
A small white room.
There was a man behind the door,
Standing upon a chair; his head
Shone honey-gold; he raised his arm
And slit my throat. I fell down dead.'

She laughed. 'The curious things we do
In dreams. I felt along my throat,
Trying to tidy it. I knew
That I was dead, so laid my coat
Over my head, because the sight
Was ugly and the floor was white.

'It seemed so lonely, then; so still;
And there was none to pity me.
I longed for pity, longed to tell
How I had died. I thought, maybe
Someone will bring a coffin soon,
And lay me in it tenderly,
And close my eyes, and mourn for me.

'Oh, how I longed for that! Some friend,
Some living friend, to see, to mind.
But then my desolation grew.
Why should the living condescend?
They seemed so different now, so strong,
So terrible, the ones I knew.

'I could not think that I had been
As splendid, beautiful as they.
The living were a world away
Beyond my servile whimpering.
For I was now a cringing thing,
A body that in terror lay,
A stupid thing with lolling head,
Meaningless, mutilated, dead.

'I thought, They must not see my shame,
Those sovereign ones. I longed to weep.
I longed to tell, but no one came.
I struggled to recall my name,
But felt the clumsy rigor creep
Into my veins, and stupefy
The remnant of my useless will;
The blood that fed my brain was dry;
I could not now remember why
I was so ugly and so still.

'Minutes, hours, years—I do not know
How much of living time passed by.
But suddenly a frightened girl
Stood on the threshold of the door.
Her eyes were fixed upon the floor.

'She did not enter the white room,
Nor move her eyes, nor come to me,
But she was of the living—she
Was of the living! That alone
Gave me new power, and I could see
Through my glassed eyes, and through the coat
That covered up my gaping throat.

'And I could speak. I cannot tell
Whether with lips and tongue. I said
"Listen! Please listen! Have you heard
Them say on earth that living men
Sometimes hear voices from the dead?"
She could not answer me, and yet
I knew she heard and understood.
"You will remember this," I said,
"For I am speaking, and am dead."

'She did not move because of fear.
"Now you must go," I said, "but when
Out of this dream you wake again,

Remember that you saw me here,
And tell the ones I loved." And then
She must have woken from her sleep
Because I watched the darkness creep
Across the door, across the room,
And seal my tomb.'

She finished and smiled up at him.
She shivered, but she was not cold.
In the bright circle of the lamp
His head shone honey-gold.

Fiona Stewart

A young poet whose work was introduced to the editors of this book by Mrs. Mary W. Findlater (p. 103), who expects fine fruit to follow blossom that has 'set' so well.

172 Quadrille

Four white birches
Dance on the hill—
Four sad daughters
In a slow quadrille;
Hidalgo-shadows
Look gravely on,
And old Duchess Moon
Is chaperone.

Watch, while she droops
Her sleeping face
Leaving their mantilla'd
Loveliness
Unprotected
For all to see!
Weaves the dance
Most delicately!

Four white birches
Dance on the hill—
Old Duchess Moon
Is sleeping still;
And still the shadows
Look gravely on
While the four sad daughters
Dance alone.

Muriel Stuart

Most poets write too much, and perhaps it is as necessary to do so as it is for a fiddler to practice every day. Muriel Stuart has certainly not published enough for the appetite of at least one reader. I first met with her work in an Anthology. Here I found a striking and tragic love-poem called 'In the Orchard'. The luckless anthologist, who was assembling *The Best Poems* of a certain year, mistakenly printed only about half the poem (enough to make me remember it), but in the following year he made amends to the even more luckless poet. We may smile a little questioningly as we read of Emma Hamilton's 'slow, divine stupidity' and then appreciate the brilliance with which a part of Nelson's complex personality is caught in the last line of the poem.

173 The Seed Shop

Here in a quiet and dusty room they lie,
Faded as crumbled stone or shifting sand,
Forlorn as ashes, shrivelled, scentless, dry—
Meadows and gardens running through my hand.

In this brown husk a dale of hawthorn dreams,
A cedar in this narrow cell is thrust;
It will drink deeply of a century's streams,
These lilies shall make summer on my dust.

Here in their safe and simple house of death,
Sealed in their shells a million roses leap;
Here I can blow a garden with my breath,
And in my hand a forest lies asleep.

174 Lady Hamilton

Men wondered why I loved you, and none guessed
How sweet your slow, divine stupidity,
Your look of earth, your sense of drowsy rest,
So rich, so strange, so all unlike my sea.
After the temper of my sails, my lean
Tall masts, you were the lure of harbour hours,—
A sleepy landscape warm and very green,
Where browsing creatures stare above still flowers.
These salt hands holding sweetness, the leader led,
A slave, too happy and too crazed to rule,
Sea land-locked, brine and honey in one bed,
And England's man your servant and your fool!
My banqueting eyes foreswore my waiting ships;
I was a silly landsman at your lips.

Helen Waddell

One of the merriest and most engaging companions with whom man or woman could dine on braised onions and burgundy, Helen Waddell began her career with a book in which she versified with great skill some of Professor Giles's translations of Chinese poetry, but she is now eminent, of course, for her sensitive and scholarly renderings of 'Mediaeval Latin Lyrics' and for her unforgettable book, *The Wandering Scholars*. She is Irish, was born in Tokio and acquired her scholarship at Oxford.

175 Appendix Vergiliana

Dancing Girl of Syria

Dancing girl of Syria, her hair caught up with a fillet;
Very subtle in swaying those quivering flanks of hers
In time to the castanet's rattle: half-drunk in the smoky tavern,
She dances, lascivious, wanton, clashing the rhythm.
And what's the use, if you're tired, of being out in the dust and the heat,
When you might as well lie still and get drunk on your settle?

Here's tankards and cups and measures and roses and pipes and fiddles,
And a trellis-arbour cool with its shade of reeds,
And somewhere somebody piping as if it were Pan's own grotto,
On a shepherd's flute, the way they do in the fields.
And here's a thin little wine, just poured from a cask that is pitchy,
And a brook running by with the noise and gurgle of running water.

There's even garlands for you, violet wreaths and saffron,
And golden melilot twining with crimson roses,
And lilies plucked where they grow by the virgin river,
—Achelois brings them in green willow baskets—
And little cheeses for you that they dry in baskets of rushes,
And plums that ripen in the autumn weather,
And chestnuts, and the cheerful red of apples.
In brief, here's Ceres, Love and rowdy Bacchus
—And red-stained blackberries, and grapes in bunches,
And hanging from his withe seagreen cucumber.
And here's the little god who keeps the arbour,
Fierce with his sickle and enormous belly.
Hither, O pilgrim! See, the little donkey
Is tired and wistful. Spare the little donkey!
Did not a goddess love a little donkey?

It's very hot.
Cicadae out in the trees are shrilling, ear-splitting,
The very lizard is hiding for coolness under his hedge.
If you have sense you'll lie still and drench yourself from your wine cup,
Or maybe you prefer the look of your wine in crystal?
Heigh ho, but it's good to lie here under the vines,
And bind on your heavy head a garland of roses,
And reap the scarlet lips of a pretty girl.
—You be damned, you there with your Puritan eye-brows!
What thanks will cold ashes give for the sweetness of melilot?
Or is it your mind to hang a rose wreath upon your tombstone?
Set down the wine and the dice, and perish who thinks of to-morrow!
—Here's Death twitching my ear, 'Live,' says he, 'for I'm coming.'

176 Petronius Arbiter

Dreams, dreams that mock us with their flitting shadows,
They come not from the temples of the gods,
They send them not, the powers of the air.
Each man makes his own dreams. The body lies
Quiet in sleep, what time the mind set free
Follows in darkness what it sought by day.
He who makes kingdoms quake for fear and sends
Unhappy cities ruining in fire,
Sees hurtling blows and broken fighting ranks
And death of kings and sodden battle fields.
The lawyer sees the judge, the crowded court,
The miser hides his coin, digs buried treasure,
The hunter shakes the forests with his hounds,
The sailor rescues from the sea his ship,
Or drowning, clings to it. Mistress to lover
Writes a love-letter: the adultress
Yields in her sleep, and in his sleep the hound
Is hot upon the traces of the hare.
The wounds of the unhappy in the night
Do but prolong their pain.

177 MS. of Benedictbeuern

To you, consummate drinkers,
  Though little be your drought,
Good speed be to your tankards,
  And send the wine about.
Let not the full decanter
  Sleep on its round,
And may unheard of banter
  In wit abound.

If any cannot carry
  His liquor as he should,
Let him no longer tarry,
  No place here for the prude.

No room among the happy
 For modesty.
A fashion only fit for clowns,
 Sobriety.

If such by chance are lurking
 Let them be shown the door;
He who good wine is shirking,
 Is one of us no more.
A death's head is his face to us,
 If he abide.
Who cannot keep the pace with us,
 As well he died.

Should any take upon him
 To drink without a peer,
Although his legs go from him,
 His speech no longer clear,
Still for his reputation
 Let him drink on,
And swig for his salvation
 The bumper down.

But between god and goddess,
 Let there no marriage be,
For he whose name is Liber
 Exults in liberty.
Let none his single virtue
 Adulterate,
Wine that is wed with water is
 Emasculate.

Queen of the sea we grant her,
 Goddess without demur,
But to be bride to Bacchus
 Is not for such as her.
For Bacchus drinking water
 Hath no man seen;
Nor ever hath his godship
 Baptized been.

Sylvia Townsend Warner

It would not be rash to predict that no one, following the carefully drawn effects with which this poem is contrived, will anticipate the wry but amusing 'twist' at the end.

178 Willow

Catkins, by village folk,
'Tis called, and after, palm;
Whose pewter fur rose-flushed
Sprays gold-dust and smells balm;

Lovely on countryside—
First hatched of all the brood
Spring mothers on the brown
Nest of the English wood;

And lovely in London too,
A greeting seeming beyond all
That envoy flowers have brought
Authentic and personal

(As we, should one beloved
Offer a keepsake, choose
No rarity but what's most
Made his by wont to use);

For man has untaught the flowers
Their first obedience,
But in a willow branch
There can be no pretence.

I with such word of Spring
By the old brown man was plied,
Who with slouched hat, and stick,
And tousled and sad-eyed

Dog at his slow heels,
Wanders through streets and squares,
With king cups sometimes, or groundsel,
Or russet wild pears.

Said I, close to my breath
Holding the willow wands:
'In sheltered woodlands now,
Or growing beside ponds,

There must be boughs a'plenty,
With their catkins putting out.'
And as I spoke I was glad;
For it seemed beyond doubt

That Spring, the swallow, was come,
And that under her sky
All men would be happy, though none
Should taste such joy as I.

Me narrow-hearted, how
His honest answer chid!
'Yes, it's too common now
To fetch the price it did.'

Mary Webb

Her verses were held in high esteem by Harold Monro, the poet of the 'twenties who kept 'The Poetry Bookshop', and she had some success as a writer of West-Country novels which may have been somewhat influenced by Thomas Hardy. Soon after her death, Earl Baldwin of Bewdley, a Prime Minister who loved both literature and England, suddenly gave her reputation an upward bound, which might have surprised as much as it would have rejoiced her.

179 Why?

Why did you come, with your enkindled eyes
And mountain-look, across my lower way,
And take the vague dishonour from my day
By luring me from paltry things, to rise
And stand beside you, waiting wistfully
The looming of a larger destiny?

Why did you with strong fingers fling aside
The gates of possibility, and say
With vital voice the words I dream today?
Before, I was not much unsatisfied:
But since a god has touched me and departed,
I run through every temple, broken-hearted.

Winifred Welles

Here is a sonnet which contrives not to recall the sonnets of early and famous poets. Perhaps the sentiment in the poem is symptomatic of an approaching era when universal compassion will be less rare than it is to-day.

180 Cruciform

Here, in the sand, where some one laid him down,
The one known human signature is clear.
Whether woman or man, white-skinned or brown,
Whether the outflung arms were so for fear
Or agony or weariness or shame,
Here, in one line athwart another line,
Is briefly written the one, mutual name,
A saviour's, or a thief's, or yours or mine.
Dunes sifted undersea long since have borne
This self-same cross, small and anonymous;
Tan deserts, that the wind has not yet worn,
Will print the symbol. And not one of us,
But then, or some day, could lie down and fit
Our desolate arms and bodies into it.

Dorothy Wellesley

The first of these poems by the Duchess of Wellington proves that a good painter may completely misjudge the temperament of a younger artist. In 1922, meeting my old painting master, Wilson Steer, I asked, 'Is there anyone at the Slade School now who has outstanding talent?' He answered, 'A boy named Rex Whistler—but he won't take anything seriously.' The Duchess's moving elegy creates a very different impression.

181 In Memory of Rex Whistler

Leave him, sweet Eros, give him peace at last.
His long, his great despair, his blood, are cast
In a rough, war-scarred, unforgotten tomb.
Only his friends remember
His gaiety, his merriment, his wit,
His art and his swift mind, pointing warm thought
With satire, learned, elegant and fit;
The tragic mask, the eyes,
One blue, the other grey.—
As Shelley saw, he saw
Himself, at ghostly four o'clock of the morning,
Standing outside in the street, his lamp still burning,
And he still drawing, drawing.
Resolved, he went the way the heroes went.

Sleep on, dear Rex, whispering 'I am content
With immortal peace, that finds at last a rest
Upon the ultimate Breast.'

182 Late Love

Should he but offer thee in part
Half-dreams of former time,
Great woman, fold him to thy heart
In his great need of later years,
When passion's not sublime.

Forgive! who never felt the whole
Love-impulse of the mind—
Fold to thy heart his broken years,
Believe! the passion of the soul
Was made for humankind.

Antonia White

The author of this powerful poem ('Epitaph') is another writer who is best known as a novelist. The resonance of these lines has something of Elizabethanism in it.

183 Epitaph

By man came death;
Not by my love, my single sun,
Did this seed ripen to its monstrous bloom
But by the moon's unquickening breath
I was undone.

Bury me deep
Lest my love look on me asleep
And see the time-stained face with which I died.
This hasty, swollen mask of yellow wax
Which fear, the clumsy workman, botched me up
Blasphemes death's patient marble.
Calmer my living brow,
Purer my cheek that flushes now
With dark decay like rouge.
I wear the face of one who could not stay
For heaven's slow marriage day
That stamps me as death's whore and not his bride.

And from that greedy coupling, hour by hour,
My bastard death grew like an iron flower
Transmuting blood to metal, bone to ice
Between the abhorring thighs.

But my eternal travail is not yet.
Not till this waxen mommet turn to flesh once more
Shall I my true-born death beget.
Not yet, not yet may I put on
Majesty and corruption.

Anna Wickham

She was born at Bendigo (Australia) and, according to her characteristically laconic phrase, 'came home from Australia with the idea of writing verse; wrote some.' Here then is a pungent and energetic specimen. Anna Wickham was found in 1947 hanging from a window of her house.

184 Nervous Prostration

I married a man of the Croydon class
When I was twenty-two.
And I vex him, and he bores me
Till we don't know what to do!
It isn't good form in the Croydon class
To say you love your wife,
So I spend my days with the tradesmen's books
And pray for the end of life.

In green fields are blossoming trees
And a golden wealth of gorse,
And young birds sing for joy of worms:
It's perfectly clear, of course,
That it wouldn't be taste in the Croydon class
To sing over dinner or tea:
But I sometimes wish the gentlemen
Would turn and talk to me!

But every man of the Croydon class
Lives in terror of joy and speech.
'Words are betrayers,' 'Joys are brief'—
The maxims their wise ones teach—

And for all my labour of love and life
I shall be clothed and fed,
And they'll give me an orderly funeral
When I'm still enough to be dead.

I married a man of the Croydon class
When I was twenty-two.
And I vex him, and he bores me
Till we don't know what to do!
And as I sit in his ordered house,
I feel I must sob or shriek,
To force a man of the Croydon class
To live, or to love, or to speak!

Margaret Willy

The work which you are about to examine is an outstanding witness that there is nothing feeble, wan or slope-shouldered in the poetry of modern women; but it is not difficult to find in it valuable touches of keen feminine perception. Without using a string of well-worn adjectives (a temptation which I have tried to avoid throughout these notes) I cannot swiftly express my own admiration for Margaret Willy's majestic verse or my high hope of her literary future; but it is likely that the reader will agree with the editor. Poetic emotion is here allied to a technique of superb quality.

185 Heathcliffe Mourns for Cathy

Put out the sun, and shroud those mocking stars,
For she is dead who lent her turbulent light
To heath and crag.
Along the snow-swept moor
Howl, you shrill wind—deafen my haunted ears
To that thin, pleading voice which all the night
Calls on me, beating at my soul's closed door.

Crouch on the hearth, and watch these embers die
Into grey ash at midnight's desolate hour.
Shut out that demon whose bewitching sin
Wheedles me with the old, enslaving cry. . . .
Heart of my bursting heart, love's tameless power
Flings back the bolt at last to let you in!

186 To a Medieval Workman: Winchester

Here, where aspiring arch or pillar raises
Its marble anthem to the timeless sky,
My thought slips back to you who wrought God's praises
With singing mind and grave, unerring eye.
I see you carving out your cosmic wonder—
Some gay device of birds or fleur-de-lys—
The teeming universe all yours to plunder
And chisel from rough stone's austerity.

Today a blind age gropes for that untainted
Vision the soul's humility discerned
Eight centuries past, when skilled hands' patient art
Shaped this saint's head, or Mary's mantle painted:
Lend us your faith-filled eyes, O you who learned
The secret wisdom of the child-like heart!

187 Dunster Church

Through the high arches dusty sunbeams stream
Gilding a bluff Elizabethan sire,
Luttrell of Somerset, whose marble dream
Marks the last winter-bed of man's desire.
Who, looking on these acquiescent hands,
Can guess the dumb hope unfulfilled, or know
What tides of spring, what green and summer lands,
Warmed the quick heart three centuries ago?

Who will remember, ninety years from now,
This August day, the heather on the hill,
Thatch in the sun . . . rich clematis . . . or how

Your seeking mind calls and mine answers still—
And all this mortal ache, burned through to be
An eyelid's flicker in eternity?

188 Gargoyles at Oxford

Malevolent or droll they brood
Ageless beneath the autumn sky:
Lugubrious minstrels, plucking lutes,
Scaled trumpeters, grotesquely sly,
Playing in cloistered haunts a dirge
For this red century's godless mood.

These watch, in frozen pantomime,
Decades of scholar-youth dream past;
Mutely they grieve—for they alone,
Half-man, half-beast, bound fast in stone,
Escape not, doomed to wear the vast
Inscrutability of time.

189 Inviolable

To the quick sense, how good feels rimy soil
Turned by the spade these steel-blue winter days;
What quiet fruitfulness the firelit toil
Shaping in solitude some rounded phrase
Or vagrant rhyme; and once, how morning-bright
First voyagings on love's enchanted main!
Yet, through this earth's chameleon delight
Perceiving One Identity shine plain.

I can look full on jagged death which sears
The warm, reluctant flesh, and wondering, know
Its impotence to cheat my youth; for still
In mortal strains the pilgrim spirit hears
News of resurgent Life, which long ago
Thwarted that nail-scarred Tree on the bleak hill.

190 The Cathedral Verger

Pacing with leisured tread the echoing nave
Between these soundless, frozen waterfalls,
He sees the fingering dawn, or winter's grave
Snowlight transfigure time-beleaguered walls;
And, wondering, knows this re-creating snow
Chiselling anew carved angel, beast or flower,
The same which lit, six centuries ago,
The cowled monk's vigil through each creeping hour.

From starry fresco, vaulted roof and pier,
From century-trodden flags beneath his feet,
They stir, and speak within his living bone—
Friends who, long dust, enslave this sentient ear,
And bind the warm heart, to its last faint beat,
To this still, sculptured loveliness of stone.

191 An Old Labourer

Here was no shivering winter, nipped and sere,
Its music muted and the sap run dry,
But the full harvest of a mellowing year
Serene beneath the late October sky.
Laden, these boughs, with fruit of toiling days:
Rough jest, an evening pipe with some staunch friend;
A lover's wonder in the fields' quiet ways
Burning still clearer here at autumn's end.

Undimmed the eyes that watched slow seasons change
From cowslip days to mist and woods aflame,
Till seventy years rolled back towards his birth;
The harvest ripe, he feared in death no strange
Dark enemy—but, calm when twilight came,
Lay down to join his old, first love, the earth.

Ursula Wood

According to my information, this poet will not for a long time fall into the sere and yellow leaf. She is fortunate, as I once was, in finding so venturesome a publisher as Mr. Basil Blackwell. There is in 'Lazarus' a verbal melody and a freshness of imagination, applied to an old theme, which ought to delight any percipient reader.

192 Lazarus

We waited in the quivering heat for his return.
None of us had seen a miracle before but we believed
in the man, and his accredited acts, We were not deceived.
he did return.

We had thought, simply, that we should all rejoice,
gathering round him, strangely unchanged by the days
he had been dead in the dark, then go on our various ways
having heard his voice.

But when he came it seemed cold as night, and we fled,
having seen fear in his terrible eyes, and great despair.
We could not break into his isolation, nor did we dare
hear what he said.

But his sisters stayed unguessing, being blinded by joy,
they took his hands and kissed them, and led him inside.
In a day or two they forgot he had ever died
or had changed since he was a boy.

ENVOI

THIS BOOK IS intended to be a salute to the brains, the sensibility and the fine artistry of women-poets. We hope that the book may help in its own measure to scrape off some of the absurd associations that seem still to cluster like barnacles round the melodious word 'feminine'.

I wish it were possible to believe that all the living writers who are here represented (thanks to their courtesy) will be satisfied by the notes which I have set under their names. I would ask them to realise three things: first, that it would have been out of place for me to criticise their work, as though I were once more adjudicating a diction class; second, that a continual stream of commendation would have become monotonous and might have sounded condescending; and third, that of necessity I am more familiar with the work of some poets, especially those whom I know personally, than with that of others.

CLIFFORD BAX

* * *

INDEX OF AUTHORS